University of California Publications

GEOLOGICAL SCIENCES

Volume 132

Quaternary Evolution and Biogeography of the Large South American Canidae (Mammalia: Carnivora)

Annalisa Berta

University of California Press

Quaternary Evolution and Biogeography of the Large South American Canidae (Mammalia: Carnivora)

Annalisa Berta

UNIVERSITY OF CALIFORNIA PRESS

Berkeley • Los Angeles • London

UNIVERSITY OF CALIFORNIA PUBLICATIONS IN GEOLOGICAL SCIENCES

Editorial Board: Stanley M. Awramik, William A. Clemens,
Richard Cowen, James A. Doyle, Peter M. Sadler

Volume 132
Issue Date: November 1988

UNIVERSITY OF CALIFORNIA PRESS
BERKELEY AND LOS ANGELES, CALIFORNIA

UNIVERSITY OF CALIFORNIA PRESS, LTD.
LONDON, ENGLAND

ISBN 0-520-09960-5
LIBRARY OF CONGRESS CATALOG CARD NUMBER: 88-23378

Library of Congress Cataloging-in-Publication Data

Berta, Annalisa.
    Quaternary evolution and biogeography of the large South American
Canidae (Mammalia, Carnivora) / by Annalisa Berta.
        p.   cm. — (University of California publications in
geological sciences; v. 132)
    Bibliography: p.
    ISBN 0-520-09960-5 (alk. paper)
    1. Canidae, Fossil—South America—Geographical distribution.
2. Canidae—South America—Evolution. 3. Paleontology—Quaternary.
4. Paleontology—South America. I. Title. II. Series.
QE882.C15B46 1988
569'.74–dc19   88-23378
                                                    CIP

Contents

Acknowledgments

This study was initiated as a Ph.D. dissertation in the Department of Paleontology, University of California, Berkeley. I am indebted to Dr. W. A. Clemens, thesis chairman, and Drs. D. E. Savage and J. L. Patton, committee members, for their critical readings of the manuscript. Discussion of the data and review of the manuscript by Dr. R. H. Tedford, C. A. Repenning, and B. E. Taylor have considerably improved the text.

Specimens in Argentine museum collections were studied during May and June 1977. The late Prof. Guillermo del Corro, Head of the Section of Fossil Vertebrates, and Dr. Jose Gallardo, Director, provided me with working space in the Paleontology Department of the Museo Argentino de Ciencias Naturales "Bernardino Rivadavia," Buenos Aires. Similar courtesies and permission to study collections were extended by Prof. Rosendo Pascual of the Natural Sciences faculty and Museo de la Universidad Nacional de La Plata, and Sr. Galileo J. Scaglia, Director of the Museo Municipal de Ciencias Naturales, de Mar del Plata. Dr. Alfredo Langguth of the Biology Departament of the Universidade Federal da Paraiba, Joao Pessoa, Brazil, provided useful suggestions through our discussion of South American canid evolution and biogeography.

I am grateful to the following individuals for the loan of
specimens and/or access to museum records: Dr. Lawrence G. Barnes,
Los Angeles County Museum of Natural History; Dr. Robert Hoffstet-
ter, Institute de Paleontologie, Museum National d'Histoire
Naturelle, Paris, France; Dr. C. S. Churcher, Department of
Zoology and Royal Ontario Museum, University of Toronto, Ontario,
Canada; Prof. G. de Beaumont, Museum d'Histoire Naturelle, Geneva,
Switzerland, and Dr. Ella Hoch, Zoologiske Museum, Copenhagen,
Denmark.

Line drawings were skillfully prepared by Mrs. J. P. Lufkin,
Staff Artist, and epoxy casts which greatly aided taxonomic
identification were provided by Mrs. Barbara T. Waters, both of
the Museum of Paleontology, University of California, Berkeley.

Financial support was provided by a University of California
Board of Regents Fellowship, 1976-77; Annie M. Alexander Scholar-
ship, 1977-78; University of California Grants-in-Aid, 1978 and
1979; and supplemental funds from the Department and Museum of
Paleontology, University of California, Berkeley. Travel to
Argentina was made possible by a National Science Foundation
Doctoral Dissertation Improvement Grant (no. DEB 7709729), and
museum work was supported by a grant from the Joseph Henry-Marsh
Fund of the National Academy of Sciences.

Finally, I would like to acknowledge the continued support and
encouragement of my parents and family.

Abbreviations

The following abbreviations are used for institutions:

AMNH Department of Vertebrate Paleontology, American Museum of Natural History, New York

EPN Escuela Politecnica Nacional, Quito, Ecuador

MACN Museo Argentino de Ciencias Naturales "Bernardino Rivadavia," Buenos Aires

MG Museum d'Histoire Naturelle, Geneva, Switzerland

MLP Museo de la Universidad Nacional de La Plata, Argentina

MMP Museo Municipal de Ciencias Naturales y Tradicional de Mar del Plata, Argentina

MNHN Museum National d'Histoire Naturelle, Paris, France

ROM Royal Ontario Museum, University of Toronto, Ontario, Canada

UCMP University of California Museum of Paleontology, Berkeley

UCMVZ University of California Museum of Vertebrate Zoology, Berkeley

UF Vertebrate Paleontology Collection, Florida State Museum, University of Florida, Gainesville

UZM L P.W. Lund Collection, Universitets Zoologiske Museum, Copenhagen, Denmark

VF Geology Department, Universidad Central, Caracas, Venezuela

YPM Yale Peabody Museum, New Haven, Connecticut

Measurements and statistics are abbreviated as follows:

C.V.	coefficient of variation	TL	talonid length
L	length	TrL	trigonid length
N	sample size	TrW	trigonid width
O.R.	observed range	TW	talonid width
S	standard deviation	W	width
TBL	trigon basin length	$\bar{X}$	mean

Abstract

Knowledge of South American large canids is summarized, new material is described, taxa are revised, and phylogenetic relationships are assessed using cladistic methodology.

The large canids discussed include dog- and wolf-sized members of the group representing Canis Linnaeus, 1758; Theriodictis Mercerat, 1891; Protocyon Giebel, 1855; and Chrysocyon Hamilton Smith, 1839 (Canidae:Caninae). This group is well documented from deposits ranging in age from Uquian (early Pleistocene) through Holocene and distributed in Argentina, Bolivia, Brazil, Ecuador, Peru, and Venezuela. Allocation of Protocyon to the subfamily Simocyoninae is rejected. Canis (Theriodictis) L. Kraglievich is referred to Theriodictis Mercerat. Three lineages of large canids are represented. The Canis lineage includes three species: C. dirus Leidy, 1858; C. gezi L. Kraglievich, 1928; and C. nehringi (F. Ameghino, 1902), and shows close affinity with North American Pleistocene Canis species. The Theriodictis-Protocyon lineage includes T. platensis Mercerat, 1891; T. tarijensis (F. Ameghino, 1902:236); P. orcesi Hoffstetter, 1952; P. scagliarum J. L. Kraglievich, 1952; and P. troglodytes (Lund, 1839b), and is most closely related to the South American fox complex comprised of Dusicyon, Pseudalopex (including Lycalopex), Cerdocyon, Atelocynus, and Speothos. The Chrysocyon lineage includes an undescribed species from the Blancan of southern North America (Tedford and

Taylor, pers. commun., 1982) and the living species C. brachyurus
(Illiger, 1815). Chrysocyon is most closely related to Canis.

The biogeographic history of these lineages is largely a
dispersal event which occurred after establishment of the Panamanian land bridge approximately 3 million years before the present
(mybp). Derived members of the Canis lineage evolved in Eurasia
and North America and subsequently dispersed into South America,
where they are first recorded from the middle Pleistocene and became extinct at the end of the Pleistocene. The Theriodictis-
Protocyon lineage is first recorded from the early Pleistocene of
South America and may reflect a prior as-yet-unrecorded history in
southern North America or Middle America. Chrysocyon evolved in
North America during the late Miocene/early Pliocene (Tedford and
Taylor, pers. commun. 1982) and is first recorded in South America
during the middle Pleistocene.

During the Pleistocene, the large canids and felids ecologically replaced a predaceous dog-like marsupial family, the Borhyaenidae. Members of the Canis and Theriodictis-Protocyon lineages
occupied the large and intermediate-sized carnivore adaptive zone
inhabited today by large felids. The Maned Wolf Chrysocyon
occupied the large and intermediate-sized omnivore zone during the
Pleistocene, in addition to the bear Arctodus and the procyonids
Cyonasua, Brachynasua, and Chapalmalania. Chrysocyon and the
spectacled bear Tremarctos survive today as the sole representatives of this zone. The small omnivore-carnivore zone is represented today as in the Pleistocene by small canids, including the
bush dog Speothos, the foxes Cerdocyon and Dusicyon, and the
small-eared dog Atelocynus. Additional occupants of this zone
include felids, procyonids, and mustelids.

Introduction

The appearance of the Panamanian land bridge linking North and South America ended South America's long history of isolation. The exact timing of this connection is, however, disputed. The geologic and invertebrate paleontologic records tend to favor a late Miocene (early Pliocene of previous workers: Nygren, 1950; Parodiz, 1969) connection. Opinions based on analyses of Recent faunal diversity and fossil occurrence of immigrant mammalian groups range from late Miocene (early Pliocene of previous workers: Hershkovitz, 1966, 1969, 1972) to late Pliocene (early Pleistocene of previous workers: Simpson, 1950; Patterson and Pascual, 1972).

Among mammalian groups involved in this interchange were placental carnivores which ecologically replaced their marsupial counterparts, the Borhyaenidae of South America (Marshall, 1978). The earliest known placental carnivores in South America, the procyonids of North American origin, first appear in Argentina in the Huayquerian (late Miocene) in a level immediately below a unit dated at 6.0 mybp (Marshall et al. 1979). Presumably they arrived prior to the appearance of the land bridge in the Pliocene (approximately 3 mybp) and dispersed along island arcs across the Caribbean region.

The Canidae, also introduced from North America, are first recorded in beds of Montehermosan (early Pliocene) age in

Argentina. However, local stratigraphy relative to this date is disputed. A questionable Chapadmalalan (late Pliocene) record of Canis gezi has been reported from landslide deposits that range in age from Chapadmalalan to Ensenadan (medial Pleistocene). Discounting these uncertain records, representatives of the group have been found in deposits which range in age from Uquian (early Pleistocene) to Holocene in Argentina, Bolivia, Brazil, Ecuador, Peru, and Venezuela.

As used here, dog- and wolf-sized members of the Canidae are referred to as the large South American canids and include Canis Linnaeus, 1758; Protocyon Giebel, 1855; Theriodictis Mercerat, 1891; and Chrysocyon Hamilton Smith, 1839 (Canidae:Caninae).

A principal objective of this study is the systematic revision of Pleistocene members of this group, using cladistic methodology. A second concern is delineation of the biogeographic history of the group. A final objective is the definition and comparison of late Cenozoic and present-day occupation of carnivore adaptive zones in South America.

HISTORICAL REVIEW OF CLASSIFICATION
OF SOUTH AMERICAN LARGE CANIDS

F. Ameghino (1889) included polyprotodont marsupials, Insectivora, Creodonta, Pinnipedia, and Carnivora in the tribe Sarcobora, which supposedly included all carnivorous mammals. He recognized the following families in the order Carnivora: Canidae, Subursidae (=Procyonidae), Ursidae, Mustelidae, and Felidae.

South American large fossil representatives of the family Canidae recognized by F. Ameghino (1902) included the genera Canis, Dinocynops, Macrocyon, and Palaeocyon (Table 1). Fossil species assigned to Canis by F. Ameghino (1889, 1902) are excluded from further discussion, since they are now recognized as species of the small fox genera Dusicyon and Pseudalopex (Berta, in prep.)

Macrocyon was diagnosed by F. Ameghino (1889:307) principally on the basis of its large size, short and robust limbs, and large entepicondylar foramen on the humerus; Dinocynops was character-ized as having a short rostrum, elevated frontals, and a large quadrate M^1 with well defined cusps (1902:232). Lund (1840a:49; 1843:53) characterized Palaeocyon as having only a hypoconid on the M_1 talonid; other canids possess an entoconid and hypoconid. Later, F. Ameghino (1904:122) recognized Amphicyon argentinus as a new creodont species which he placed in the Amphicyoninae and which he differentiated from canids in the size and orientation of the principal cusps.

Revilliod (1924a) revised F. Ameghino's nomenclature and suggested that Macrocyon and Dinocynops should be synonymized under Palaeocyon, and that species of Palaeocyon and Canis (fide Lydekker, 1894) should be grouped under the subgenus Canis (Palaeocyon). By 1926, Revilliod was convinced that all of the genera and species of large canids in the South American fossil record should be referred to P. troglodytes, though his diagnosis of Palaeocyon was more general in scope than that provided by Lund (1843).

The first comprehensive review of the large South American fossil canids was presented by L. Kraglievich (1928). He recognized Canis (= Dinocynops, Macrocyon) and Palaeocyon, and proposed a new subgenus Canis (Theriodictis), similar to both Canis and Palaeocyon but differentiated from the latter by the presence of an entoconid on M1. He also transferred Amphicyon argentinus to the genus Canis. The taxonomic arrangement of Canis used here follows that of L. Kraglievich with one exception. The subgenus Theriodictis has been removed from the genus Canis and elevated to generic level.

In a later classification, L. Kraglievich (1930) recognized, in addition to the Caninae, the subfamily Cyoninae. Within this latter subfamily he included the living genera Speothos (Bush Dog, Central and South America), Cuon (Dhole, Asia), Lycaon (Hunting

TABLE 1
Taxonomic arrangement of subfamilies
and genera of South American large canids

F. AMEGHINO, 1902	P. REVILLIOD, 1926
Family Canidae	Family Canidae
Subfamily Caninae	Subfamily Caninae
Dinocynops	Palaeocyon (sensu lato)
Macrocyon	
Palaeocyon	

L. KRAGLIEVICH, 1930	J. L. KRAGLIEVICH, 1952
Family Canidae	Family Canidae
Subfamily Caninae	Subfamily Caninae
Canis	Canis
Canis (Theriodictis)	Canis (Theriodictis)
Chrysocyon	Chrysocyon
Subfamily Cyoninae	Subfamily Simocyoninae
Palaeocyon	Protocyon

THIS STUDY

Family Canidae
 Subfamily Caninae
  Canis
  Theriodictis
  Protocyon
  Chrysocyon

Dog, Africa), and the fossil genus Palaeocyon. The subfamily Cyoninae was diagnosed by absence of the metaconid on M_1, absence of M_3, reduction of M^2, and simplification of M^1.

Simpson (1945:107), following Giebel (1855:851), made Palaeocyon a junior synonym of Protocyon and placed it within the subfamily Simocyoninae (=Cyoninae), along with a number of European and North American Tertiary genera and the three living genera Speothos, Cuon, and Lycaon. J. L. Kraglievich (1952) followed Simpson's 1945 arrangement, recognizing the Simocyoninae and the genus Protocyon.

Diagnosis of the Simocyoninae is based on the presence of a trenchant talonid on M_1. This unicuspid condition differs from the bicuspid condition of the Caninae in having the hypoconid enlarged and crest-like and the other talonid cusps reduced. Because of the independent and parallel development of this character in other carnivore groups (Hough, 1948; Thenius, 1954), alliance of genera to this subfamily on the basis of this character has been questioned.

Bueler (1973) reaffirmed earlier suggestions that Lycaon, Speothos, and Cuon have nothing specific in common except this tooth character, and pointed out a few differences that illustrate this lack of relationship. Cuon and Speothos show reduction in number of teeth; however, Lycaon does not. The pollex or dew claw is absent in Lycaon but present in Cuon and Speothos. While Cuon and Lycaon are relatively large and long-legged animals, Speothos is small and short-legged. Speothos, like two other South American indigenous canids, Chrysocyon and Cerdocyon, has a short, straight caecum rather than the long, coiled caecum common to most other canids, including Lycaon and Cuon.

Clutton-Brock, Corbet, and Hills (1976) performed a numerical analysis on members of the family Canidae, using a combination of anatomical and behavioral characters. They concluded that subfamilial separations are not warranted and noted that Speothos, Cuon, and Lycaon are monotypic, highly specialized genera whose similarity to one another is too low to justify a subfamilial level of relationship.

Tedford (written commun., 1968) suggested that fossil genera originally included in the Simocyoninae can be divided among at least two and possibly three other families in addition to the

Canidae. I have removed Protocyon from the subfamily Simocyoninae
and placed it within the subfamily Caninae (Table 1).   This
family-level taxonomic arrangement is supported by features of the
auditory region and basicranium.

SOUTH AMERICAN LATE CENOZOIC LAND MAMMAL AGES

The chronology and usage of South American land mammal ages in
this study (Fig. 1) follows that proposed by Marshall et al.
(1982; 1979).   From oldest to youngest, respectively, the Uquian,
Ensenadan, and Lujanian land mammal ages are presently included
within the Pleistocene, with the Uquian straddling the boundary
between   epochs   (Patterson   and   Pascual,   1972;   Patterson   and
Fidalgo, 1972).   The Chapadmalalan, Montehermosan and early and
middle Uquian land mammal ages comprise the currently restricted
Pliocene.   Berggren and Van Couvering's (1974) radioisotopic time
scale and definition of epoch boundaries correspond with the
Miocene-Pliocene boundary placed at 5.0 mybp and that of the
Pliocene-Pleistocene placed at 1.8 mybp.
   The historical development of temporal and faunal nomenclature
for the Plio-Pleistocene of South America is summarized elsewhere
(Marshall et al., 1984, fig. 1). Criteria for recognition of these
South American late Cenozoic land mammal ages is provided by Pascual et al. (1967) and Marshall et al. (1984). The ages recognized
were originally defined on the basis of Argentine deposits and
faunas, specifially those within the Province of Buenos Aires.
Each land mammal age has as its means of recognition a characteristic association of genera, together with first and last records
of occurrence of certain taxa.   It should be realized that these
characterizations are tentative and subject to future refinements.
Undoubtedly, as the late Cenozoic of Argentina, indeed, that of
the entire continent, becomes better known, the recognized geo-
chronologic duration of many of these land mammal genera will
change.

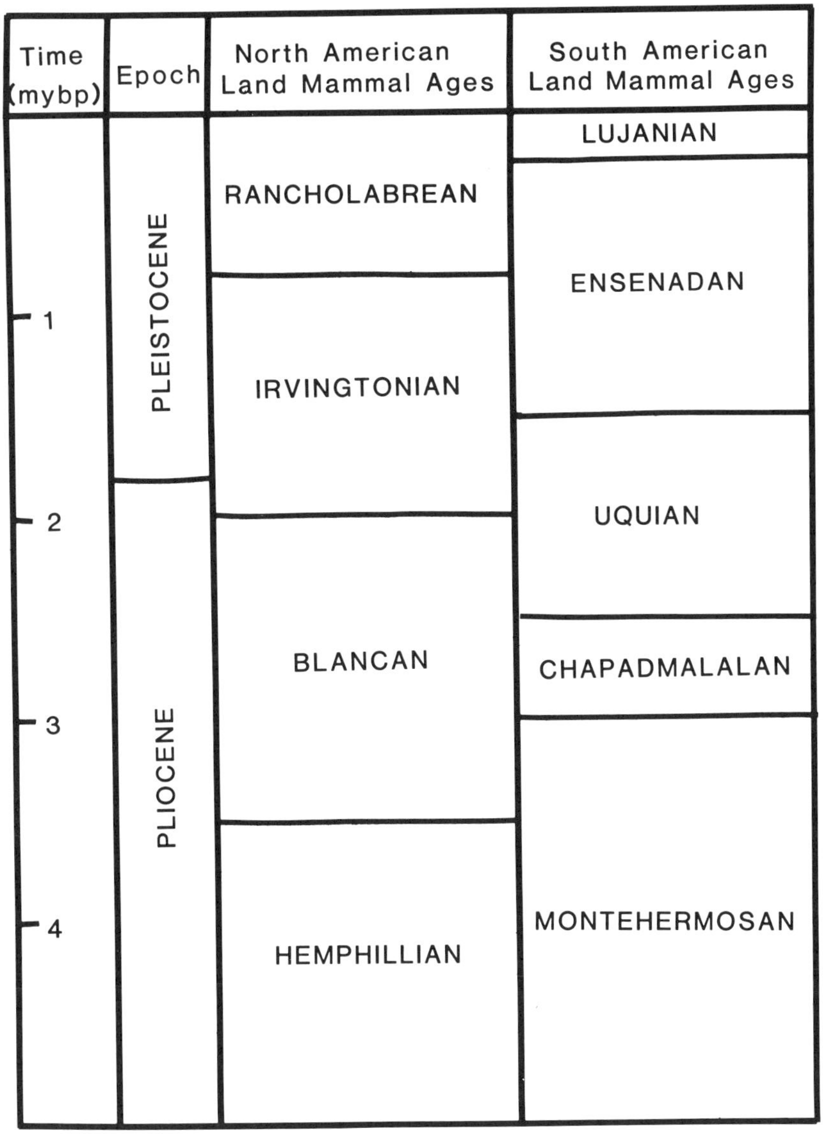

Time (mybp)	Epoch	North American Land Mammal Ages	South American Land Mammal Ages
			LUJANIAN
	PLEISTOCENE	RANCHOLABREAN	ENSENADAN
1		IRVINGTONIAN	
2			UQUIAN
		BLANCAN	CHAPADMALALAN
3	PLIOCENE		
4		HEMPHILLIAN	MONTEHERMOSAN

FIGURE 1. Correlation of North and South American late Cenozoic land mammal ages, following Marshall, et al. (1982).

Radioisotopic age determinations of rocks associated with late Cenozoic mammal-bearing beds and calibration of land mammal ages in terms of a radioisotopic time scale, as has been done for North America and Europe (Evernden et al., 1964), have only recently become available for South America (Marshall et al., 1979, 1982; MacFadden et al., 1983). Prior to the work of Marshall et al., (1979), only two late Cenozoic radioisotopic dates were known. These dates, 5.5 and 6.4 mybp, were reported from a basal tuff ("Toba 76") from the Umala Formation, south of La Paz, Bolivia (Evernden et al., 1966). Fossil mammals have been reported from beds conformably overlying this tuff. A tentative Montehermosan age for this fauna has been suggested by Hoffstetter and Villarroel (1974).

Marshall et al., (1979) report a series of K/Ar dates and magnetostratigraphic data from late Tertiary mammal-bearing beds in the Catamarca Province of northwest Argentina which allow for refinement of duration and boundaries of beds of Chasicoan (medial Miocene) through Chapadmalalan (late Pliocene) age. Of interest is a 3.55 mybp date they report for a tuff collected near the top of Corral Quemado Formation at Puerta de Corral Quemado. A tentative Montehermosan age has been assigned to a fauna recovered from the upper part of this formation (Riggs and Patterson, 1939). Mammal faunas collected from the type Uquian land mammal age (Uquia Formation, Jujuy Province, northwestern Argentina) and calibrated by radioisotopic and paleomagnetic determinations indicate that these sediments range in age from 2.5 (late Pliocene) to 1.5 mybp (early Pleistocene) (Marshall et al., 1982).

Correlation of late Cenozoic South American and North American land mammal ages is based largely upon mutual exchange of taxa, which together with the radioisotopic chronology suggest the following correlations (Fig. 1): Lujanian with medial and late Rancholabrean, Ensenadan with late Irvingtonian, Uquian with Irvingtonian and latest Blancan, Chapadmalalan with late Blancan, and Montehermosan with early and medial Blancan and late Hemphillian (Marshall et al., 1982).

STRATIGRAPHY, AGE, AND INTRACONTINENTAL CORRELATIONS

In Argentina, as elsewhere, stratigraphic nomenclature has been confused by frequent usage of the same terminology for lithostratigraphic units (e.g., formation), chronostratigraphic units (e.g., stage-age), and biologic units (e.g., fauna). The fact that the most natural divisions of rock, time, and faunal units frequently do not coincide explains the resultant confusion in attempting to represent them by a single system of nomenclature.

In the Pampean region of Argentina, extending from the pampas of Buenos Aires to the Chaco Plains, there are three classic areas where combined geologic and paleontologic studies of Pleistocene deposits and faunas have been made: (1) Buenos Aires city and environs (including La Plata and Ensenada, Buenos Aires Province) (F. Ameghino, 1875-1909); (2) the coastal cliffs between Mar del Plata and Miramar (Buenos Aires Province) (J. L. Kraglievich, 1952); and (3) cliffs along the south bank of the Rio Parana (Entre Rios Province) (L. Kraglievich, 1930). These deposits comprise the Pampean Group, which consists of 50-80 meters of subeolian, fluvial, and lacustrine silty sands, and partly loessoid sediments with interbedded tuffites and clays (Harrington, 1956:153). Faunas collected from these areas have provided the stratigraphic framework for the characterization of late Cenozoic land mammal ages.

Unfortunately, most previous workers in these areas did not recognize formations (sensu American Commission on Stratigraphic Nomenclature, 1961). They were more concerned with biologic characterization of the contained faunas. F. Ameghino (1906) grouped late Cenozoic deposits from Argentina into a single rock unit, the "Pampean Formation".   He subdivided this "formation" into a series of biologic units, "pisos" (from oldest to youngest- -Ensenadense, Belgranense, Bonaerense, and Lujanense).   These "pisos" were distinguished on the basis of the stage of evolution of their mammal faunas.   F. Ameghino (1906) grouped late Cenozoic deposits from Argentina into a single rock unit, the "Pampean Formation."   He subdivided this "formation" into a series of biologic units, "pisos" (from oldest to youngest -- Ensenadense, Belgranense, Bonaerense, and Lujanense).   These "pisos" were distinguished on the basis of the stage of evolution of their mammal faunas.   He later recognized the time significance of these associations of taxa and attempted to redefine "pisos" as bio-stratigraphic units, thereby extending his faunal correlations of sediments throughout Argentina.

The "Pampean Formation" is now considered synonymous with the Pliocene and Pleistocene.   Although operationally defined on the basis of contained faunas, other workers have used this unit as a chronostratigraphic or lithostratigraphic unit, and definitions have changed according to these different criteria.   For this reason, difficulties in attempting to unify these definitions were encountered.

Reference to this name in this study bears no relation to the present concept of "formation" in Argentina, which is in accord-ance with that proposed in the American Code of Stratigraphic Nomenclature (1961).

Most of the large fossil canids recovered from Argentina were collected from units recognized by early workers as the "Pampean Formation."   Fossil localities in the "Pampean Formation," as recognized in this study, are all considered to be Lujanian in age, based on their faunas.   The geographic distribution of Argentine Pleistocene localities discussed below is shown in Figs. 2, 3, and 4.

Subsequent to F. Ameghino's work, geologic and stratigraphic work in Buenos Aires has led to recognition of the following mammal-bearing formations, listed here from oldest to youngest, together with their previous temporal (fide F. Ameghino, 1889) means of recognition: Ensenada Formation (Ensenadense), Buenos Aires Formation (Bonaerense), and Lujan Formation (Lujanense). The type of Canis gezi has been recovered from one of these units, the Ensenada Formation, Ensenadan in age.

The work of J. L. Kraglievich (1952), who defined and described lithostratigraphic units in the Chapadmalal and Miramar districts of Argentina, is exemplary in its proper usage of stratigraphic nomenclature. He applied names to lithostratigraphic units previously identified only by age names. These strata range in age from Chapadmalalan through Holocene and their demonstrated superpositional relationships offer an excellent opportunity for refined correlations of land mammal ages. He has recognized the following formations, listed from oldest to youngest: Chapadmalal, Barranca de Los Lobos, Vorohue, San Andres, (San Andres member of Vorohue Formation: J. L. Kraglievich, 1959:6), Miramar, Arroyo Seco, Loberia,and Samborombon. Protocyon scagliarum and Protocyon sp. have been recovered from the Vorohue Formation, Uquian in age.

Future work should tie this closely controlled association of rocks in the Chapadmalal and Miramar districts of Argentina to the Plio-Pleistocene fossil record of North America and Europe. Attention should be paid to the separation of lithostratigraphic and paleontologic units, systematic identification and description of characterizing fossils within the strata, and delineation of the vertical ranges of taxa both in these local stratigraphic sections and with reference to their total geographic distribution.

In addition to Argentina, large fossil canids have been recovered from the Lagoa Santa Caves, Brazil; Talara, Peru; La Carolina and Guamote (near Riobamba), Ecuador; Nuapua, Tarija, Quebrada del Puente Alto (near Tarija), Boliva and Muaco, Venezuela. The geographic distribution of these localities is shown in Fig. 2. Age correlations of the non-Argentine localities discussed below are given in Fig. 5.

FIGURE 2. Map of South America showing Pleistocene vertebrate
localities (circles) and the location of Figs. 3 and 4
discussed in text.

FIGURE 3. Map of Buenos Aires, Argentina, and vicinity, showing Pleistocene vertebrate localities (circles) discussed in text.

FIGURE 4. Map of Mar del Plata, Argentina, and vicinity, showing Pleistocene vertebrate localities (circles) discussed in text.

Epoch	Countries So. Amer. L. M. Ages	BOLIVIA	BRAZIL	ECUADOR	PERU	VENEZUELA
Holo- cene						
Pleistocene	Lujanian	Ñuapua l — Quebrada del Puente Alto	Lagoa Santa	La Carolina Guamote	Talara	Muaco
Pleistocene	Ensenadan	Tarija				

FIGURE 5. Age correlation of principal non-Argentine South American faunas containing large canids.

Abundant remains of Protocyon troglodytes and a smaller sample of Chrysocyon brachyurus were recovered by the Danish naturalist Peter Lund from the Lagoa Santa Caves in the state of Minas Gerais, Brazil.   The deposits in these caves range in age from Lujanian through Holocene and were first explored by Lund, who from 1836 to 1845 collected 115 mammalian species representing 12 orders and 33 families. Unfortunately, none of this material was collected stratigraphically; the only information recorded with the specimen is the name of the cave from which it was collected.

A large sample of Canis dirus was collected from Talara, Peru, by a Royal Ontario Museum expedition in 1958.   The main bone-bearing deposits at Talara occur in tar seeps in the La Brea-Parinas oil fields, the largest being in a region about 10 miles southeast of Talara.   In addition to mammals, representatives of the classes Amphibia, Aves, and Reptilia have been reported from Talara.   The fossils were derived from irregularly alternating lenses of medium to coarse, poorly sorted, angular gravels and crossbedded sands (Lemon and Churcher, 1961; Churcher, 1959, 1962, 1965; Churcher and Zyll de Jong, 1965; Hoffstetter, 1970).   A Lujanian age for the fauna has been proposed by these authors.

Protocyon orcesi was established on the basis of specimens collected by F. Spillmann from La Carolina on the Santa Elena Peninsula, Ecuador. According to Hoffstetter (1952), the material was apparently recovered from fluviatile sediments.   He proposed the name "Carolinien" for this faunal association, which includes plant and insect remains as well as reptiles, birds, and a diverse mammalian fauna.   From its stratigraphic position, the Carolinien fauna is Lujanian in age.

E. Torres and R. J. Hoffstetter collected a single specimen referred to P. troglodytes in 1976 from Guamote   (50 km south of Riobamba), Chimborazo Province, Ecuador.   According to Hoffstetter (pers. commun., 1978), the associated Lujanian fauna includes Glossotherium, Palaeolama, and Equus.

Specimens referred to Theriodictis platensis were collected from Tarija, Bolivia, by F. de Carles in 1888 for the Museo Argentino de Ciencias Naturales "Bernardino Rivadavia" in Buenos Aires. Unfortunately, their precise locality is not known.   Known collections of this fauna have come from various stratigraphic levels (Hoffstetter, 1963a, b; MacFadden and Wolff, 1981; MacFadden et al., 1983) and are Ensenadan and possibly Lujanian in age. The fauna is clearly younger than typical Ensenadan faunas, but older than Lujanian-age faunas of Argentina.   For the present, the most reasonable suggestion is that of L. Kraglievich (1930, 1934), who favored placement of the Tarijan fauna in the hiatus (=Bonaerense) between these two ages.   Hoffstetter collected several   other   specimens   from   Tarija   that   are   referred   to Theriodictis, T. cf. T. tarijensis and Theriodictis sp. MacFadden and Wolff collected material representing two individuals re-ferable to P. troglodytes in the Tarija basin in the summer of 1979.

Hoffstetter and Galarza in 1965 collected a specimen referred to _Canis dirus_ from Quebrada del Puente Alto (6 km southeast of Tarija. A tentative Lujanian age for this fauna has been proposed (Hoffstetter, pers. commun., 1978).

A specimen referable to _P. troglodytes_ was collected by Hoffstetter from the lowest member of Nuapua 1. Hoffstetter (1968) reported the following mammalian families from Nuapua 1: Glyptodontidae, Dasypodidae, Megalonychidae, Megatheriidae, Mylodontidae, Hydrochoeridae, Ursidae, Felidae, Macraucheniidae, Toxodontidae, Gomphotheriidae, Equidae, and Camelidae. MacFadden and Wolff (1981) on the basis of additional faunal and paleomagnetic data, report a late Lujanian/Holocene age for this site.

Remains of _Canis dirus_ have been recovered in muds 2-3 meters thick from a water-hole site at Muaco, Falcon State, Venezuela. The Muaco fauna, described by Royo y Gomez (1960), Bryan (1973:245), and Boquentin (1979), includes Reptilia, Aves, and a diverse mammalian fauna. ^{14}C dates reported for the Muaco fauna range from $9,030^+$ 240 (IVIC-488) to $16,375^+$ 400 (0-999) mybp. (Bryan, 1973:244).

TABLE 2

Cranial, Mandibular, and Some Cheek Tooth Measurements of South American Large Canids

Specimen	Length	Greatest Length	Zygomatic Width	Braincase Width	Maxillary Toothrow Length	Maximum Skull Width across Cheek Teeth	Palatal Width (C^1)	Frontal Shield Width	Post-orbital Constriction	Length M^2-Bulla	Height Maxillary Toothrow-Orbit	Jugal Depth	P^4 Length	Bulla Length	Rostrum Length	P^4-M^2 Length	Length of Mandible	Length of Toothrow	Height of Mandible	Depth of Mandible Below M_1	Length M_1
Canis dirus																					
ROM 2053	217.2	307.5	166.8	69.7	104.5	—	—	80.4	45.5	76.1	42.3	21.5	31.0	30.2	96.9	53.8	—	—	—	—	—
ROM 4303	—	—	159.9	68.3	102.7	96.7	39.2	84.6	63.6	79.9	43.9	21.4	29.7	29.5e	—	50.3	—	—	—	—	—
VF-?	—	311.6e	160.0e	72.2	—	—	*34.0	34.0	49.1	—	—	21.3	31.2	—	—	—	—	—	—	—	—
Canis gezi																					
MACN 5120	197.0	252.0	130e	75.5	92.3	86.5	35.8	64.8e	54.6e	60.0	35.0	18.2	27.6	29.4	79.6	49.2	—	130.0	—	33.2	30.8
Canis nehringi																					
MACN 500	199.0	256.0	155.3	75.6	89.4	87.0	33.6	76.0	49.0	60.4	33.7	20.3	27.5	29.4	86.0	48.3	159.2	120.0	70.9	31.7	28.7
Theriodictis platensis																					
MLP 10-51	180e	—	—	55.5	82.5	87.2	34.3	73.3e	46.5	59.0	28.6	17.2	25.7	22.6e	60e	43.4	171.8e	112.3e	67.7	28.6	28.0
MG 634/14	188e	—	—	62e	88e	87	37.5	68.0	48.5	57.5	38.5	22.5	27.7	—	—	46.0	—	—	72.5	35.0	—
Theriodictis tarijensis																					
MACN 1452	202.2	260.0	—	58.3	86.4	—	34.6	—	—	68.4	—	15.3	26.8	26.1	68.7	45.0	—	—	—	29.5	—
Protocyon scagliarium																					
MMP 164	170.0	214.3	126.3	58.9	78.9	75.5	28.0	50.2	44.5	53.2	29.4	15.3	25.0	25.9	65e	42.7	—	82.6	60.0	28.0	24.8

METHODS

A series of cranial and dental measurements were taken on the specimens studied.   The cranial measurements are those used by Tedford and Taylor (pers. commun., 1978), with several additions (Table 2); descriptions are listed below and illustrated in Figs. 6 and 7.   All measurements are given in millimeters (mm) unless otherwise specified; accuracy is to the nearest 0.1 mm.   Estimated measurements are followed by "e."

Cusp terminology used in the descriptions and illustrated in Fig. 8 follows Van Valen (1966:8, fig. 1).

Specimen illustrations were based upon epoxy casts and photographs; the UCMP number following the original specimen number refers to the cast.   Casts have been deposited in the Vertebrate Collections, Museum of Paleontology, University of California, Berkeley.

Cranial Measurements

1. Length, posterior C/ to foramen magnum notch distance from posterior border of canine alveolus to foramen magnum notch.
2. Greatest length—length from anterior tip of premaxillae to posterior point of inion.
3. Zygomatic width—greatest distance across zygomata.
4. Braincase width—maximum breadth of braincase across level of parietotemporal sutures.
5. Maxillary toothrow length—distance from anterior edge of alveolus of P^1 to posterior edge of alveolus of M^2.
6. Maximum skull width across cheek teeth—greatest breadth between outer sides of most widely separated upper teeth (P^4 or M^1).
7. Palatal width at P^1—minimum width between inner margins of alveoli of first upper premolars.

8. Frontal shield width-maximum breadth across postorbital processes of frontals.

9. Postorbital constriction least-width across frontals at constriction behind postorbital processes.

10. Length, M^2 to bulla-minimum distance from posterior edge of alveolus of M^2 to depression in front of bulla.

11. Facial depth, maxillary toothrow to orbit-minimum distance from alveolar margin of M^1 to most ventral point of orbit.

12. Jugal depth-minimum depth of jugal anterior to postorbital process, at right angles to its anteroposterior axis.

13. P^4 length-maximum anteroposterior length of crown measured on outer side.

14. Bulla length-length from median lacerate foramen to suture of bulla with paroccipital process.

15. Rostrum length-length from anterolateral margin of infraorbital canal to anterior tip of premaxillae.

16. Length P^4 to M^2-maximum distance between outer sides of P^4 to M^2.

17. Length of Mandible-distance from posterior edge of alveolus of I^1 to posterior edge of angular process.

18. Mandibular toothrow-length distance from anterior edge of alveolus of canine to posterior edge of M_2 or M_3.

19. Height of mandible-maximum distance between highest point of coronoid process and base of angular process perpendicular to the toothrow.

20. Depth of mandible below M_1-distance from alveolar margin of M_1 at protoconid to ventral border of mandible transverse to long axis of ramus.

21. M_1 length-maximum anteroposterior length of crown, measured on outer side parallel to long axis of ramus.

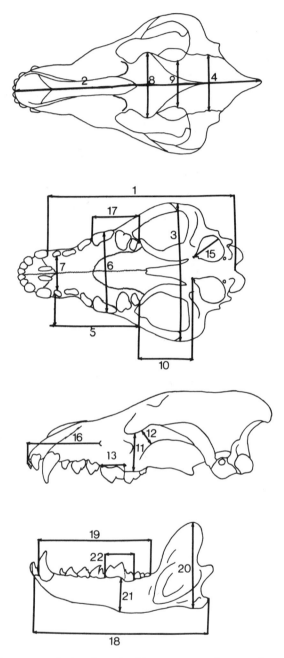

FIGURE 6. Diagram of _Canis_ skull and mandible, illustrating cranial and mandibular measurements.

Tooth Measurements

1. Upper incisors, canines, and premolars.
   a. Maximum length—measured on labial side.
   b. Maximum width—measured at right angles to length.

2. P^4.
   a. Maximum length.
   b. Protocone width—maximum distance from protocone to anterolabial extremity of tooth.

3. M^{1-2}.
   a. Maximum length—distance from anterior margin of the paracone to posterior margin of the metacone.
   b. Maximum width—distance from labial margin of the anterolabial corner of the crown to lingual margin of the tooth.
   c. Trigon basin length—maximum distance across trigon.

4. Lower incisors, canines, and premolars.
   a. Maximum length.
   b. Maximum width—measured at right angles to length.

5. M_{1-2}.
   a. Maximum length—distance from anteriormost point on the paraconid to posterior margin of the talonid.
   b. Trigonid and talonid width—widest part of these portions of the crown, measured at right angles to length.
   c. Trigonid length—distance from anteriormost point on the paraconid to posterior margin of the protoconid or metaconid.
   d. Talonid length—distance from posterior margin at the base of the metaconid to posterior margin of the talonid.

6. M_3.
   a. Maximum length.
   b. Maximum width—measured at right angles to length.

A

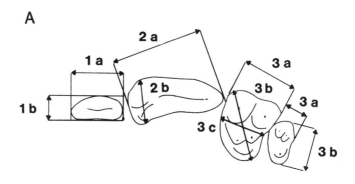

B

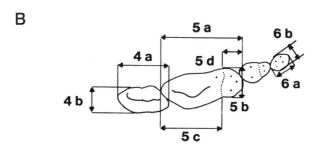

FIGURE 7. Diagram of upper (A) and lower (B) dentition of
Canis, illustrating tooth measurements.

CHARACTER ANALYSIS

Determination of phylogenetic relationships among the South
American Pleistocene large canids in this study was based upon
cladistic methodology (Henning, 1966). Characters were selected
and their polarity (either primitive or derived) evaluated. The
goal of character evaluation is discovery of the level of hierarchy at which a character evinces a shared derived similarity,
and therefore defines a set of taxa as monophyletic. Initially, I
considered three methods for the evaluation of character polarity:
commonality, fossil record, and outgroup comparison.

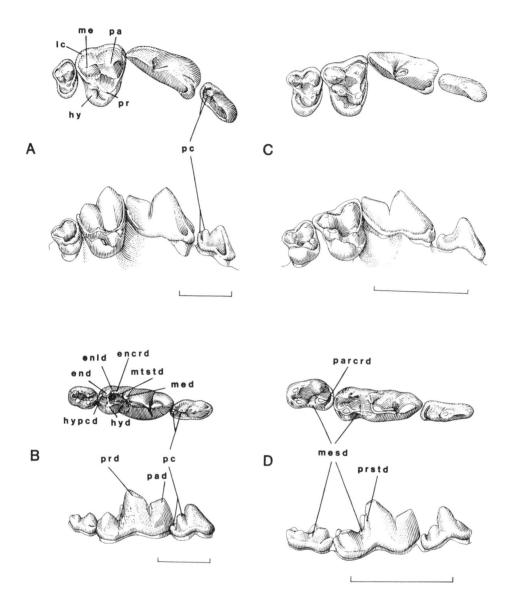

FIGURE 8. Left upper (A) and lower (B) dentition of Canis
dirus, and left upper (C) and lower (D) dentition of Pseudalopex
culpaeus, illustrating dental nomenclature. Scale = 20 mm.
Abbreviations as follows:

encrd	entocristid	me	metacone	parcrd	paracristid
end	entoconid	med	metaconid	pc	posterior
enld	entoconulid	mesd	mesoconid		cusplet(s)
hy	hypocone	mtstd	metastylid	pr	protocone
hyd	hypoconid	pa	paracone	prd	protoconid
hypcd	hypoconulid	pad	paraconid	prstd	protostylid
lc	labial cingulum				

The "commonality principle," a traditional and widely used approach, involves examination of the frequency distribution of a character. The rationale is that a character that is widespread in a group is likely to be primitive for that group, advanced characters having a more limited distribution. This method was rejected for this analysis, since it requires a great many initial assumptions (e.g., equal rates of evolution). Without other criteria such as ontogenetic sequences or outgroup comparison, it is impossible to differentiate those instances where "common" equals "primitive" from those where it does not (see Watrous and Wheeler, 1981; Nelson, 1978).

Use of the fossil record to assess character polarity involves examination of the distribution of a character in time and the recognition of primitive and derived characters, based on their stratigraphic record. A weakness of this approach is that it is based on two questionable assumptions: (1) that the fossil record being used is sufficiently complete to determine polarity, and (2) that characters that occur earliest are necessarily primitive. Given these a priori assumptions, I have in those instances where information from the stratigraphic record conflicted with data derived from outgroup comparison (as e.g., in comparison of the phylogenetic and stratigraphic records of Protocyon and Canis Figs. 27-28) invoked the outgroup method to resolve the problem.

Outgroup comparison proved the most objective method of polarity evaluation, since it is based upon the fewest number of assumptions. This method involves mapping the distribution of a character within a group and within a larger set of close relatives, the outgroup. Determination of derived characters is based on the parsimony criterion, which requires the fewest character transformations (originations and losses) to account for a distribution pattern. Use of this methodological criterion is advocated by Wiley (1975:236) "not because nature is parsimonious, but because only parsimonious hypotheses can be defended by the investigator without resorting to authoritarianism or a priorism."

Another aspect of cladistic analysis involves a system of "weighting" characters once their polarity has been determined (Hecht, 1976; Hecht and Edwards, 1976). This approach is consistent with the traditional view that some characters are especially useful in assessing phylogenetic relationship, whereas others probably represent convergences or parallelisms. Consequently, a cladogram based on characters readily subject to convergences or parallelism is less likely to be correct than one which is based on evolutionary novelties. However, as Eldredge and Cracraft (1980) discuss, the assumption that characters which comprise an integrated functional complex should be given more weight, as they are less likely to represent a convergence or parallelism, is seriously flawed, since it assumes a priori which features are more likely to have evolved more than once and at what level in the hierarchy that occurred. This so-called "Form-Function" information is, however, useful in other nonphylogenetic contexts, especially as concerns the ecologic habitus occupied by the animal.

I have selected for evaluation principally cranial and dental characters. In most instances, associated skeletal material was lacking. Interpretation of the polarity of character-states (-, primitive; +, derived), defined below and listed with their functional significance (where known), is based upon Tedford and Taylor's (pers. commun., 1978) comprehensive study of the North American Canini, in which the most significant outgroup comparisons were made with a primitive North American canid, "Canis" davisi, known from the Hemphillian. Outgroup comparisons were also made with Vulpes and Leptocyon, taxa more distantly related to "Canis" davisi. Advanced living South American canids Dusicyon, Pseudalopex (including Lycalopex), Cerdocyon, Atelocynus, and Speothos and the large fossil genera Theriodictis and Protocyon, form a monophyletic group (Berta, 1981). Within this group Cerdocyon, Atelocynus, and Speothos, together with the Asian raccoon dog Nyctereutes, form a distinct clade. Chrysocyon

is excluded from this group and is most closely related to Canis
(see section on Phylogenetic Relationships).

SKULL

1. Frontal sinus absent (1-), or present (1+).

Development of the frontal sinus in canids is varied, and
three derived character-states are recognized among the South
American canids considered here (Fig. 9):

1+, a. Frontal sinus large, does not penetrate postorbital
process (as in Protocyon and Dusicyon, Pseudalopex,
and Cerdocyon).

1+, b. Frontal sinus large, penetrating postorbital
process, extending anteriorly and particularly
posteriorly ultimately to the frontal-parietal
suture (as in Canis, Chrysocyon, and Theriodictis).

1+, c. Frontal sinus small, does not penetrate postorbital
process (as in Speothos and Atelocynus).

1+, a.
1- -->1+   1+, b.
1+, c.

The primitive condition, lack of a frontal sinus, is shown by a
groove or shallow depression on the dorsal surface of the
postorbital process and is the common condition among Leptocyon
and Vulpes. Presence and expansion of a frontal sinus among
advanced canids is reflected in the form of the postorbital
process. The significance of pneumatization in the canid skull is
not well understood, although it has been related to olfaction,
since the sinus usually has secondary linings formed by
ethmoturbinates (Evans and Christensen, 1979).

2. Zygomatic arch-relatively shallow zygomata, and masseteric
scar unpronounced (as in most advanced canids) (2-). Deep
zygomata and wide masseteric scar (as in Theriodictis,
Protocyon, and Dusicyon australis) (2+).

2- --> 2+

3. Zygomatic arch-moderately arched or nearly flat zygomata with an everted or shelf-like jugal (as in "Canis" davisi) (3-). Strongly arched zygomata with inverted jugals (as in all other advanced canids) (3+).

3- --> 3+

The zygomatic arch provides an attachment surface for the temporalis and masseter muscles; its architecture is therefore involved in the mechanics of jaw closure.

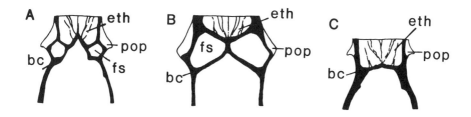

FIGURE 9. Diagram showing the derived states of the frontal sinus (ventral view of frontal section) in some advanced canids: (A) Psuedalopex vetulus, (B) Canis latrans, and (C) Speothos venaticus. Natural size. Abbreviations as follows:
bc   anterior wall of basicranium
eth   ethmoidal labyrinth
fs   frontal sinus
pop   postorbital process

4. Supraoccipital shield-rectangular, fan-shaped shield with a rounded convex apex (as in "Canis" davisi, C. gezi) (4-). Narrow, triangular shield (as in C. nehringi, C. dirus) (4+).

4- --> 4+

The temporalis muscle extends and inserts onto the supraoccipital shield, also affecting jaw closure.

5.   Palatines-short palatines extending to or just anterior to
     the toothrow (as in most advanced canids) (5-).   Two derived
     character-states (5+) are recognized:
       5+, a. Long palatines extending to or beyond toothrow (as
              in Theriodictis, Protocyon, Dusicyon).
       5+, b. Very short palatines not extending to toothrow (as
              in Cerdocyon).

                         5- --> 5+, a.
                              5+, b.

6.   Palate-narrow (6-) or palate wide (6+).   This character is
     expressed by the ratio of palate width to skull length.   The
     derived condition is recognized among advanced canids,
     including C. gezi, C. dirus, C. nehringi, C. cf. C. dirus,
     Theriodictis, Protocyon, and Dusicyon australis.

                         6- --> 6+

7.   Anterior lacerate foramen and optic foramen-in separate
     openings (as in most Canis species) (7-), or in common
     opening (as in C. dirus, C. nehringi) (7+).

                         7- --> 7+

8.   External auditory meatus-proportional to bulla length (as in
     most advanced canids) (8-), or very short with small diameter
     (as in Cerdocyon, Nyctereutes, Speothos, and Atelocynus)
     (8+).

                         8- --> 8+

MANDIBLE
9.   Subangular lobe-absent (9-), or present (9+).

                         9- --> 9+

Huxley (1880:251) first described this large, rounded, bony flange
beneath the angular process, though he did not discuss its
function. Development of a subangular lobe is seen among the South
American living canids Speothos and Cerdocyon, the Asian raccoon
dog Nyctereutes, the African Bat-Eared Fox Otocyon, and the Gray

Fox Urocyon, and is less well developed in Protocyon.   The
digastric muscle, responsible for opening the jaw, inserts on the
subangular lobe.   Ewer (1973:42) suggested that its line of action
is altered in those genera possessing the lobe.   The insertion is
shifted back to a point above the glenoid, which greatly increases
the muscle's efficiency as a jaw opener. A jaw mechanism of this
sort would be advantageous for quick repetitive chopping, as one
would expect from an insectivorous diet.

10.   Angular process slender, attenuated, and with a dorsal hook,
      inferior pterygoid fossa not expanded (Type A of Gaspard,
      1964, fig. 24) (as in "Canis" davisi) (10-).   Large, with
      expanded fossa for inferior/superior branches of medial
      pterygoideus muscle or expanded pterygoid fossa (as in
      advanced canids) (10+).   Three derived character-states are
      recognized among the South American canids discussed here
      (Fig. 10):

      10+, a. Angular process large, usually blunt, without
              dorsal hook, fossa for inferior branch of medial
              pterygoideus muscle expanded (Type B of Gaspard,
              1964, fig. 24) (as in Theriodictis, Protocyon,
              Dusicyon, and Pseudalopex).

      10+, b. Angular process with pterygoid fossa greatly
              expanded (Type D of Gaspard, 1964, fig. 24) (as in
              Cerdocyon, Nyctereutes, Atelocynus, and Speothos).

      10+, c. Angular process with large fossa for superior
              branch of medial pterygoideus muscle (Type C of
              Gaspard, 1964, fig. 24) (as in Canis and
              Chrysocyon).

                    10+, a. --> 10+, b.
              10-
                    10+, c.

Gaspard (1964) detailed functional aspects of the different types
of angular process.   She recognized laceration (carnivore-shear),

trituration (omnivore-grinding), and intercuspidation (insectivore-chopping) as major masticatory groups, each characterized by a different type of angular process. South American large canids can thus be divided into (1) a laceration group (Theriodictis, Protocyon) and (2) a laceration-trituration group (Canis, Chrysocyon). This character, in its association with the masticatory functional complex, is very useful in allowing one to discriminate between dietary specializations, and ultimately, based on this, to infer different ecologic roles for the various genera.

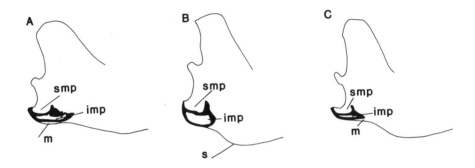

FIGURE 10. Diagram showing the derived states of the angular process (medial view) in some advanced canids:
(A) Pseudalopex culpaeus, (B) Cerdocyon thous, and
(C) Canis latrans. Natural size. Abbreviations as follows:

imp   insertion of inferior branch of M. pterygoideus internus
m   insertion of M. masseter superficialis
s   subangular lobe
smp   insertion of superficial branch of M. pterygoideus internus

It was also found to have considerable importance in phylogenetic differentiation of these genera.

11. Coronoid process anteroposteriorly narrow and dorsoventrally high (as in Canis and Chrysocyon) (11-), or anteroposteriorly broad and dorsoventrally low (as in Theriodictis, Protocyon, Dusicyon, Cerdocyon, Nyctereutes, Atelocynus, and Speothos) (11+).

$$11- \longrightarrow 11+$$

The temporalis muscle inserts on the coronoid process of the mandible, as far down as the ventral margin of the masseteric fossa. Its function is to raise the mandible in closing the mouth. Presumably, the shape of the process reflects the relative size of the temporalis muscle.

DENTITION

12. I^3-small, without posteromedial cingulum (as in Leptocyon and Vulpes) (12-), or enlarged (12+). Two derived character-states are recognized: I^3 enlarged, with strong posteromedial cingulum (as in "Canis" davisi, Dusicyon, Theriodictis(?), and Protocyon). I^3 enlarged, with accessory cusps and strong posteromedial cingulum (as in Canis and Chrysocyon).

$$12- \longrightarrow 12+, a \longrightarrow 12+, b.$$

13. Premolars-elongate and low-crowned (13-), or short and high-crowned (13+).

$$13- \longrightarrow 13+$$

Among the South American large canids this derived character-state is found in Protocyon, where it is associated with the trend toward hypercarnivory (see characters 20, 22, 26 and 27).

14. Premolars-simple, without posterior cusplets (as in Leptocyon and Vulpes) (14-), or complex, with posterior cusplets (as in advanced canids) (see Fig. 9) (14+)

$$14- \longrightarrow 14+$$

15. P^4/M_1-large relative to M^{1-2}/M_{2-3} ("macrodont," <u>sensu</u> Huxley, 1880:248) (15-), or small relative to M^{1-2}/M_{2-3} ("microdont," <u>sensu</u> Huxley, 1880:248) (as in <u>Chrysocyon</u> and <u>Cerdocyon</u> clade) (15+). The derived condition is figured by Langguth (1969:122, fig. 28).

15- --> 15+

16. P^4 The derived condition is figured by Langguth (1969:122, fig. 28) with large, high protocone, anterolingual orientation, and sharp anterolabial border (16-). With reduced, low protocone, posterolingual orientation, and rounded anterolabial border (16+).

16- --> 16+

Most canids display a relatively large protocone, a strongly anterolingually directed protocone, and a sharp anterolabial tooth border. All advanced canids described herein show the derived condition, which includes reduction and posterolingual orientation of the protocone and rounding of the anterolabial tooth border. In the <u>Theriodictis-Protocyon</u> lineage, the derived trend culminates in the very reduced protocone characteristic of <u>Dusicyon australis</u>.

17. M^{1-2}-wide for their length (17-), or very narrow for their length (17+). The derived condition is recognized in <u>Cerdocyon</u>, <u>Nyctereutes</u>, <u>Atelocynus</u>, <u>Speothos</u>, and <u>Chrysocyon</u>.

17- --> 17+

18. M^{1-2} paracone and metacone-nearly equal (as in "Canis" davisi) (18-), or paracone larger (as in all advanced canids) (18+).

18- --> 18+

19. M^{1-2} labial cingulum-well developed (19-), or reduced (19+).

19- --> 19+

A strongly developed labial cingulum is retained among some advanced canids (e.g., <u>Canis dirus</u>). The derived condition, a trend toward eventual loss of the labial cingulum, is shown by other advanced canids (<u>C</u>. cf. <u>C</u>. <u>dirus</u>, <u>C</u>. <u>gezi</u>) and by <u>Cuon</u> and <u>Lycaon</u>.

20. M^{1-2} hypocone-large (20-), or reduced (20+).

20- --> 20+

Reduction of the M^{1-2} hypocone is a feature related to the trend toward hypercarnivory seen in Protocyon. Simplification of the M_{1-2} talonid by reduction or loss of the metaconid and entoconid is reflected in the morphology of its opposing teeth, specifically M^{1-2} talon basins. Members of the Canis lineage show development of two distinct talon basins: protocone basin and hypocone basin; in occlusion, the hypoconid fits into the protocone basin while the entoconid occupies the hypocone basin. Reduction of the metaconule and hypocone among Protocyon affects morphology of the talon basin. The talonid is usually slender and comprised of a large piercing hypoconid, which in occlusion occupies the talon basin. The very reduced entoconid, consisting only of a basal cingular shelf, shears past the very reduced hypocone shelf.

21. M^{1-2} hypocone-posterolingual relative to the protocone (as in most advanced canids) (21-), or anterolingual relative to the protocone (as in C. gezi) (21+).

21- --> 21+

22. M^{1-2} hypocone-large (as in most advanced canids) (22-), or reduced (as in Theriodictis and Protocyon) (22+).
    Two derived character-states are recognized:
    22+, a. M^{1-2} hypocone reduced to shelf.
    22+, b. M^{1-2} hypocone very reduced or absent.

22- --> 22+,a --> 22+,b

23. M^2 metacone-relatively unreduced (as in most advanced canids) (23-), or reduced (as in Theriodictis and Protocyon) (23+).

23- --> 23+

24. M^{1-2} anterolingual cingulum-complete, extending around protocone (as in most canids) (24-), or incomplete (as in C. dirus, C. nehringi) (24+).

24- --> 24+

25. P_3 crown-when viewed laterally oriented vertically (as in most advanced canids) (25-), or with posterior tilt

(as in Theriodictis, Protocyon, and Dusicyon) (25+).

25- --> 25+

26. P_4 posterior cusplets-absent (26-), or present (26+).

Two derived character-states are recognized:

26+, a. P_4 with second posterior cusplet.

26+, b. P_4 with anterior and posterior cusplet.

26- --> 26+, a --> 26+, b.

The advanced canids, including Theriodictis and Canis have developed a second posterior cusplet behind the principal cusp (26+, a.).   Character state 26+, b. is found among the Protocyon lineage (P. scagliarum), and in the African hunting dog Lycaon and the Asian dhole Cuon.   It is associated with other characters of hypercarnivory including short, high-crowned premolars and a simple talonid.

27. M_{1-2} tricuspid trigonid and bicuspid talonid (27-).

Two derived character-states (27+) are recognized.

27+, a.   Hypocarnivory: complex trigonid and talonid.

27+, b.   Hypercarnivory: simple trigonid and talonid.

27+, a.

27- --> 27+

27+, b.

Most canines exemplify the plesiomorphic condition: presence of a tricuspid trigonid (paraconid, protoconid, and metaconid) and a bicuspid talonid with a large hypoconid and smaller entoconid, usually not joined by a transverse crest.   Two derived trends, hypocarnivory and hypercarnivory are recognized among advanced canids.   The hypocarnivorous trend (27+, a.) is displayed by some Canis species (e.g., C. dirus) and includes enlargement and complication of cusps on the trigonid and talonid.   The hypercarnivorous trend (27+, b.), illustrated by Theriodictis and Protocyon species, includes simplification of the trigonid and talonid and involves reduction and ultimate loss of the metaconid and entoconid.   Several transformation states of the simple trigonid and talonid can be defined: 27+, b-1 metaconid absent; talonid

bicuspid (entoconid present as distinct cusp), 27+, b-2 metaconid
absent; talonid unicuspid (entoconid absent).

$$27+, \text{b-1.} \longrightarrow 27+, \text{b-}_2.$$

28. M_1 protostylid absent (28-), or present (28+).

$$28- \longrightarrow 28+$$

Among South American canids, the Dusicyon clade, excluding
Theriodictis and Protocyon, are all characterized by the presence
of a small cusp, the protostylid on the labial margin of the
protoconid (see Fig. 8).

29. M_{1-2} mesoconid absent (29-), or present (29+).

$$29- \longrightarrow 29+$$

South American living canids, excluding Urocyon, are all characterized by the presence of a small cusp, the mesoconid on the
crista obliqua of M_{1-2} anterior to the hypoconid (see Fig. 8).

30. M_2 anterolabial cingulum-extending to hypoconid (30-), or
reduced (as in advanced canids) (30+).

$$30- \longrightarrow 30+$$

31. M_2^2-proportionally smaller than M_1^1 (as in advanced canids)
(31-), or considerably smaller than M_1^1 (as in Theriodictis,
Protocyon, and Dusicyon) (31+).

$$31- \longrightarrow 31+$$

32. M_2 paracristid-weak or absent (as in Canis) (32-), or strong
(as in Theriodictis, Pseudalopex, Protocyon, Dusicyon) (32+)
(see Fig. 8).

$$32- \longrightarrow 32+$$

33. M_2 metaconid-reduced (as in Canis) (33-), or unreduced (as in
Theriodictis, Protocyon, and Dusicyon) (33+).

$$33- \longrightarrow 33+$$

34. M^2/M_3-present (34-), or absent (34+).

$$34- \longrightarrow 34+$$

The extant Bush Dog, Speothos venaticus, exemplifies the derived
condition. Protocyon orcesi conserves in part the derived
condition, having lost the M_3 but retaining the M^2.

OTHER CHARACTERS

35. Ears-long (35-), or short (35+).

35- --> 35+

Clutton-Brock et al., (1976:189, table 7) define this character, ear length, as percentage of length of head and body. In Nycterentes, Atelocynus, Cerdocyon, and Speothos ear lengths range between 8-10% of head and body length. Other canids range between 9-25%.

36. Caecum-long and convoluted (36-), or short and straight (36+).

36- --> 36+

Polarity of this character is given in Clutton-Brock, et al., (1976:191, table 8). Cerdocyon, Nycterentes, Speothos, and Chrysocyon show the derived state.

37. Limbs proportional to body size (as in Canis and Dusicyon) (37-).

Two derived states (37+) are recognized.

37+, a. Limbs greatly elongate (as in Chrysocyon).

37+, b. Limbs very short (as in Cerdocyon,
          Nycterentes, Atelocynus, and Speothos).

37+, a.
37- --> 37+
37+, b.

This character was modified from Hildebrand (1952:fig. 14) and Clutton-Brock et al., (1976:191, table 8), who list it as length of hindlimbs and forelimbs as percentage of body spine length. Chrysocyon has a hindlimb 103% and forelimb 92% of body spine length, compared with Canis, which ranges between 73-79% for hindlimbs and 62-71% for forelimbs. Cerdocyon, Nycterentes, Atelocynus, and Speothos have a hindlimb between 58-69% and forelimb between 52-59% of body length.

SYSTEMATICS

Order Carnivora Bowdich, 1821
Superfamily Canoidea Simpson, 1931
Family Canidae Gray, 1821
Subfamily Caninae Gill, 1872
Genus Canis Linnaeus, 1758

Synonymy of South American Taxa:

Macrocyon F. Ameghino, 1881:306.

Dinocynops F. Ameghino, 1902:232 (partim).

Stereocyon Mercerat, 1917b:17.

Canis (Palaeocyon) Revilliod, 1924a:2 (partim).

Palaeocyon Revilliod, 1926:11 (partim).

Aenocyon Merriam, 1918:532.

Canis (Aenocyon) Stock, Lance, and Nigra, 1946:109.

Type specimens. Macrocyon robustus F. Ameghino, 1881:109.
Stereocyon nehringi Mercerat, 1917b:17. Aenocyon dirus Merriam,
1918:532.

Geographic distribution. Fossil species from Argentina, Bolivia,
Peru, and Venezuela.

Age. Montehermosan (? - early-medial Pliocene), Ensenadan (medial
Pleistocene), and Lujanian (late Pleistocene).

Included South American species. Fossil representatives of the
genus Canis include C. dirus, C. gezi, and C. nehringi.

Revised Diagnosis. Frontal sinus large, penetrating postorbital
process and extending posteriorly to the frontal-parietal suture
(Fig. 9); strongly arched zygomata with inverted jugal; I^3
enlarged with accessory cusps and strong posteromedial cingulum;
P^4 with reduced protocone, posterolingually directed with well
rounded anterolabial border; $M1^{-2}$ with large hypocone; coronoid

process anteroposteriorly narrow and dorsoventrally high; angular process expanded with large fossa for superior branch of medial pterygoideus muscle (Fig. 10); Ml with metaconid, large hypoconid and smaller entoconid joined by cristids to form a transverse crest; M_2 lacking paraconid with weak paracristid, reduced antero-labial cingulum, and metaconid.

Canis dirus Leidy, 1858:21
(Figs. 11-13; Plate 1)

Canis (Aenocyon) dirus, Churcher, 1959:564.

Aenocyon (?) Royo y Gomez, 1960:156.

Material. In ROM: 4303, a nearly complete skull missing lateral walls of frontals and premaxillae with right P^2, P^4-M^2 (P^1, P^3 alveoli), and left C, P^3-M^2 (P^{1-2} alveoli); ROM 2053, right half of skull with complete basicranium and right I^2, P^4-M^2 (I^1, I^3-P^3 alveoli); 2051, 2052, 6411, 6412A-C basicrania; 2047, left ramus with complete dentition; 2048, left ramus with M_{1-2} (C, P_{1-3}, M_3 alveoli); 2049, right ramus with P_3, M_{1-2} (C, P_1, M_3 alveoli, P_4 broken at base); 2050, left ramus with P_{3-4}, M_{1-2} (P_{1-2}, M_3 alveoli); 2162, right ramus with P_{3-4}, M_{1-2} (P_1, M_3 broken at crown); 2260, right ramus with C, P_{2-4}, M_{1-2} (P_1, M_3 alveoli); 3022, fragmentary left ramus with P_3-M_2 (posterior half of P_3) (P_4, M_1, M_3 alveoli); 3024, fragmentary right ramus with I_3, C, P_{1-4}, M_{1-2}; 3076, incomplete left ramus, missing ascending portion with P_{2-4}, M_{1-2}; 4301, left ramus with P_{1-4}, M_{1-2}; 4302, incomplete left ramus, missing incisor region with P_{2-4}, M_{1-2} (P_1, M_2 alveoli); 5992, right ramus with M_{1-2} (C, P_{1-4}, M_3 alveoli); 6391, right ramus with P_{3-4}, M_1, (P_1, M_3 alveoli); 6392, right ramus with P_{3-4}, M_{1-2} (C broken 9.7 mm above base, P_{1-2}, M_3 alveoli); 6393, right ramus with P_3, M_{1-2} (P_{1-2}, P_4 alveoli); 6395, right ramus with P_{3-4}, M_{1-2}, (P_{1-2}, P_3 alveoli); 6396, right ramus with P_3 (P_1 alveolus, P_{2-4}, M_{1-2} broken at crown); 6397, right ramus with P_3, anterior portion P_4, M_{1-2} (C, P_{1-2} alveoli); 6398, right ramus with P_{3-4} (C, P_1, P_3 alveoli, P_2, M_2 broken at crown); 6399, right ramus with P_{3-4}, M_1 (P_{1-2}, M_{2-3} alveoli); 6400, right ramus with M_1 (P_{1-4}, M_{1-2} alveoli); 6401 A-E, fragmentary right rami with teeth (5); 6402 A-W, fragmentary right rami with teeth (23); 6403 A-L, fragmentary right rami with teeth, posterior half to one-third (12); 6404, left ramus with M_{1-2} (C, P_{1-2}, M_3 alveoli); 6407, left ramus with P_3, M_{1-2} (I_{2-3}, C, P_{1-2}, P_4, M_3 alveoli); 6408 A-G, fragmentary left rami with teeth (7); 6409 A-W, fragmentary left rami with teeth (23), caudal vertebrae; 2101 (proximal two-thirds) bacula; 2160, 2261, 6220-6221, scapula; 2042, 2446-2450, 2567, 2657, 2865, 3007, 3008, 6105-6110, 6120, right humerus; 2041, 2043, 2451-2457, 2568, 2569, 2940, 2943, 6112-6119, left humerus; 6122, 2473 humeral fragments; 2036, 2038, 2484, 2486-2488, 2471, 2572, 2939, 3005, 6147-6149, 6151 A-O, 6153, 6154, right radius; 2035, 2037, 2039, 2489-2494, 2867, 2954, 3073, 6144, 6145, 6146, 6152, left radius; 2237, 2485 radii fragments; 2033, 2034, 2106, 2475, 2481, 2482, 2573, 3006, 3075, 6160, 6161, right ulna; 2475, 2477-2479, 2574, 3074, 6158, 6159, 6162, left ulna; 2483 A-O, ulnar fragments; 6373 A-J, right metacarpal I; 6372 A-L, left metacarpal I; 4825, 4852 (part), 4862 Y-Z (part), right metacarpal II; 4824, 4853 (part), 4862 A-B (part), left metacarpal II; 4826 A-Z, 4854 A-H (part), 4863 A-C, left metacarpal III; 4827, 4854 R-Z (part), 4863 X-Z (part), right metacarpal III; 4829 A-R, 4855 W-Z (part), 4866 Y-Z (part), right metacarpal IV; 4828, 4855 A-H (part), 4866 A-E (part), left metacarpal IV; 4831 A-T, 4856 X-Z (part), 4864 V-Z, right metacarpal V; 4830, 4856 A-F (part), left metacarpal V; 2505, 4861, metapodials; 2504, 2739, 6357, pelvis; 6359-6364, right ilium; 2497-2499, 3036, 3066, 6350, 6352, 2496, left ilium; 2495, 6358, 6366 A-R, 6365, right coxal; 6349, 6351, 6356 A-X, 6367, left coxal; 2933 A-P, 6417 A-C (fragments) sacrum; 2458-2465, 2517, 2863, 2937, 3002, 5647, 5649, 5658-5669, 5671 A-J, 5673 A-B, 5675 A-E, right femur; 2044, 2466-2471, 2566, 2914, 3003, 3004, 5648, 5646, 5650-5657, 5662, 5670 A-I, 5672 A-G, 5674 A-C, left femur; 2472, 2506, femoral fragments; 2017, 2046, 2433-2439, 2444, 2570, 2656, 2917, 3001, 3071, 3072, 6131-6134, 6136, right tibia; 2045,

2440-2443, 2910, 2918, 3054, 3080, 6127-6129, 6130-A-M, 6137 A-H, left tibia; 6143 A-X, fibulae; 6166 A-Z, 6167, right astragalus; 2502 A-Z, 2503A-K, left astragalus; 2501 A-D, 6163 A-X, left calcaneum; 2500, 6164 A-Z, right calcaneum; 4832 A-M, 4857 A-B, 4865 A-B, left metatarsal II; 4833 A-U, 4857 X-Z (part), 4865 (part), right metatarsal II; 4834 A-T, 4842 A-C, 4858, left metatarsal III; 4835 A-N, 4858 V-Z, right metatarsal III; 4837 A-P, 4841 A-Z, 4859 T-Z (part), right metatarsal IV; 4836 A-Q, 4841 A-B, 4859 A-C, left metatarsal IV; 4860 Q-Z (part), right metatarsal V; 4840 A-E, 4860 A-D, left metatarsal V; 6368, proximal phalanges; 6369, medial phalanges; 6371 A-O, distal phalanges.

AMNH 56602, right M^1, right metatarsal III.

VF ?, nearly complete skull, missing left zygomatic portion of squamosal with left I^3, C, P^2, P^4. M^{1-2} (I^{1-2}, P^{2-3} alveoli) and right I^{2-3}, C, P^{1-4}, M^{1-2} (I^1 alveolus); VF 407, right upper C; VF 988, fragmentary right maxilla with half of C, P^2 (P^1 alveolus); VF 349, right metatarsal III.

MNHN TAR-751, incomplete right ramus with P_2, M_{1-2} (I_3, C, P_1, P_{3-4} broken at crown; M_3 alveolus).

Stratigraphic and geographic distribution.   ROM specimens were collected from the La Brea-Parinas oil fields southeast of Talara, Peru, by an ROM expedition.   AMNH specimens were collected from an undesignated locality in Talara.   VF specimens were collected by Prof. Francisco Gutierrez and colleagues in 1952 from Muaco, Falcon State, Venezuela.   MNHN specimens were collected by R. Hoffstetter and H. Galarza from Quebrada del Puente Alto, 6 km southeast of Tarija, Bolivia.

Age. Lujanian.

Revised diagnosis.   Supraoccipital shield narrow with triangular apex and inion projecting beyond condyles; wide palate; anterior lacerate and optic foramen in common pit; $P^2/_2$ with posterior cusplets; P^3 with two posterior cusplets; M^{1-2} with prominent labial cingula and anteriolingual cingulum seldom extending around the protocone; P_3 with posterior cusplet; P_4 with two posterior cusplets, the second always arising on the cingular heel; M_1 with metastylid, entocristid, entoconulid, transverse crest running from metaconid to hypoconid; M_2 with entocristid and entoconulid.

Description. Knowledge of the cranium of C. dirus is based upon two nearly complete skulls from the Talaran sample (ROM 2053, 4303) and a single specimen from Muaco (VF ?). Cranial dimensions are listed in Table 2.

Greatest length of the skull averages 309.5 mm. This is considerably larger than those of C. nehringi or C. gezi. Skull width measured across the zygomatic arches is 75% of skull length and comparable to that in other South American species of Canis. Postorbital processes are large and laterally inflated, reflecting development of a large frontal sinus. The sagittal crest is uniformly high, strongly compressed and accentuated by well de- fined temporal ridges (Fig. 11). The relatively broad skull shows a marked postorbital constriction in front of the braincase which is relatively small and only slightly expanded, measuring 32% of skull length. The rostrum is long relative to skull length. A characteristic feature of this species is its wide palate. Comparison with other South American large canids indicates that C. dirus has the widest palate relative to skull length. The infraorbital foramen is situated above the anterior root of P^4.

C. dirus has a relatively deep face, measuring on the average 43 mm from the outer alveolar margin of M^1 to the most ventral point of the orbit, which is 19% of skull length. The widely flared zygomatic arch ranges from 159.9 mm to 166.8 mm dorsoventrally at its widest point, larger than that in either C. gezi or C. nehringi. The jugal is also relatively large, its depth averaging 21.4 mm, suggesting development of a large masseter muscle. In this species the attachment of the masseter muscle is very strongly marked on the inferior side of the zygomatic arch, as indicated by a prominent knot on the suture

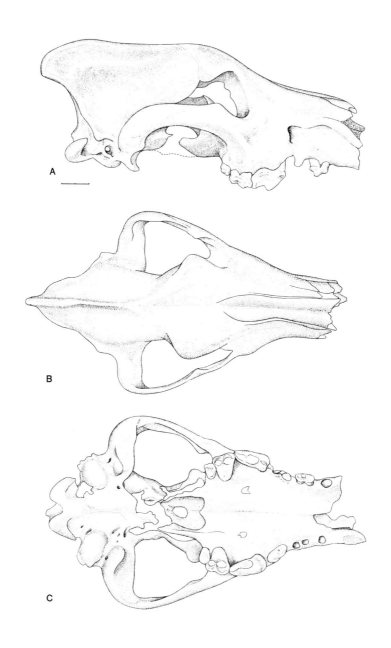

FIGURE 11. _Canis dirus_ Leidy, 1858. ROM 4303, skull: (A)
lateral, (B) dorsal, and (C) ventral views. Scale = 20 mm.

between the jugal and the maxillary. Anterior lacerate and optic foramen are joined in a common opening.

The supraoccipital shield is narrow and triangular. Lambdoidal crests are strongly developed, converging at the apex of the shield. An overhanging inion, strongly downturned and extending beyond the condyles, is typically developed (Fig. 11, Pl. 1). Bulla length averages 29.7 mm, which is only slightly larger than that of other South American Canis.

Upper tooth dimensions of Talaran and Muaco specimens are listed in Tables 3 and 4, respectively. None of the maxilla found have preserved the I^1 in association with other cheek teeth. An isolated specimen, ROM 4259, has a subtriangular occlusal outline with two basal cusps on either side of the principal cusp. The lingual basal cusp is elevated relative to the principal cusp. A strong V-shaped lingual cingulum connects the basal cusps. I^2 and I^3 are progressively larger. I^2 retains only a labial basal cusp. I^3 is caniniform and has accessory cusps and a well developed posteromedial cingulum. The canine is large, and prominent anterolingual ridges extend from the base of the crown to the apex.

P^1 is simple, single-rooted, and single-cusped; the principal cusp is slightly hooked posteriorly. P^2 is elongate and double-rooted, with a small posterior cusplet developed behind the principal cusp. The double-rooted P^3 is considerably larger than P^2, with two posterior cusplets behind the principal cusp. The second cusplet always arises on the cingular heel. Relative to M^{1-2}, P^4 is large. The protocone is small, low, and set close to the body of the tooth. A prominent ridge is present, running from the slight notch between the protocone and well rounded anterolabial extremity of the tooth to the paracone (Fig. 8). The basal lingual cingulum is varied in its development; in a few Talaran specimens it is complete and can be traced from the paracone to the metacone.

M^1 has a complete labial cingulum developed (Fig. 8). On some specimens it weakens where the bases of the paracone and

TABLE 3

Upper Tooth Dimensions of Canis dirus

	Dimension	N	O.R.	$\bar{X}$	S	C.V.
I^1	L	2	6.9 – 7.6	7.25	.494	6.813
	W	2	6.7 – 7.6	7.15	.636	8.895
I^2	L	2	8.4 – 8.7	8.55	.212	2.479
	W	2	8.2 – 8.3	8.25	.070	.848
I^3	L	2	9.8 – 10.3	10.05	.353	3.512
	W	2	7.4 – 8.3	7.85	.636	8.101
C	L	5	11.8 – 15.1	13.64	1.384	10.146
	W	5	8.5 – 11.6	10.36	1.268	12.129
P^1	L	2	9.0 – 9.3	9.15	.212	2.316
	W	2	6.1 – 6.8	6.45	.494	7.658
P^2	L	3	13.1 – 14.5	13.96	.757	5.422
	W	3	6.1 – 7.1	6.76	.577	8.535
P^3	L	2	16.1 – 18.0	17.05	1.343	7.876
	W	2	7.8 – 8.3	8.05	.353	4.385
P^4	L	9	26.9 – 31.1	28.64	1.338	4.671
	W	9	12.1 – 13.8	12.85	.665	5.175
M^1	L	11	14.9 – 18.3	17.00	1.417	8.335
	TBL	11	11.6 – 14.9	13.56	1.016	7.492
	W	12	20.5 – 24.9	23.13	1.622	7.012
M^2	L	2	9.2 – 9.3	9.25	.070	.756
	TBL	2	7.9 – 8.1	8.00	.141	1.762
	W	2	13.1 – 13.3	13.20	.141	1.068

TABLE 4

Measurements of Cheek Teeth of Canis

Upper Dentition	I¹		I²		I³		C		P¹		P²		P³		P⁴		M¹			M²		
	L	W	L	W	L	W	L	W	L	W	L	W	L	W	L	W	L	W	TBL	L	W	TBL
Canis dirus VF-?	---	---	8.3	6.2	9.8	9.7e	16.7	11.4	9.0	6.7	15.1e	7.1	17.6	7.9	31.2	13.6	18.0	21.5	---	8.4	13.5	
Canis nehringi MACN 500	6.4	3.9	8.2	6.1	---	---	12.6	9.5	8.3	6.0	13.1	5.4	15.1	6.4	27.5	12.8	16.0	21.5	12.0	8.0	12.4	
Canis gezi MACN 5120	5.0	4.6	---	---	9.6	6.6	12.5	9.0	7.5	6.0	14.5	5.7	15.0	6.6	24.8	13.2	17.7	19.0	12.0	7.8	11.7	

Lower Dentition	I₁		I₂		I₃		C		P₁		P₂		P₃		P₄		M₁					M₂			
	L	W	L	W	L	W	L	W	L	W	L	W	L	W	L	W	TrL	TrW	TL	TW	TBL	TrL	TrW	TL	W
Canis dirus MNHN TAR 751	---		---		---		17.1e	12.0	6.0	5.0	12.3	7.2	14.5	6.9	15.0e	8.8e	24.5	8.6	13.4	12.2	---				
Canis nehringi MACN 500	---		---		---		---		---		12.1	5.8	12.6	6.0	17.7	8.5	22.0	7.7	12.2	10.9	6.5	4.0	8.1	5.7	4.6
Canis gezi MACN 5120	5.0	2.9	5.9	4.5	7.7	6.5	16.7	12.9	7.8	5.0	12.2	6.0	14.3	7.0	15.5	7	23.6	7.3	12.2	10.9	---	4.5	8.7	7.2	4.7
MLP 52-IV-27	---		---		---		---		---		---		---		---		29.4	---	11.8	---	---	9.6	8.0	5.1	4.7

metacone join.   A large metaconule and smaller paraconule are
joined to the protocone by two cristae. The anterolingual
cingulum usually does not extend around the large protocone;
however, one specimen, AMNH 56602, shows a faint cingulum
extending around this cusp.   The large hypocone is posterolingually directed relative to the protocone. M^2 is reduced
relative to M^1, with a complete labial cingulum.   In some
specimens an entire cingulum is developed, encircling the tooth
(Fig. 8).   The paracone is only slightly larger than the
metacone.   A large protocone and reduced metaconule are present.
The hypocone is large and more anteriorly positioned relative to
the protocone than in M^1. The anterolingual cingulum arising at
the paraconule extends around the protocone.

The ramus is relatively long, ranging from 200 mm to 208.4
mm in the Talaran sample.   It is transversely narrow and relatively deep, particularly below M_{1-2}.   Depth of the mandible
measured below M_1 in this sample ranges from 32.2 to 37.7 mm; the
same dimension in C. gezi and C. nehringi falls near the short
end of this range.   A large mental foramen is positioned below P_1
and P_2, and a smaller foramen is located below the anterior root
of P_3.   Height of the ramus measured from the coronoid process to
the base of the ascending ramus is considerably greater than that
in other South American large canids (Table 2).   The coronoid
process is anteroposteriorly narrow and dorsoventrally high.   The
angular process is expanded dorsoventrally, with a slight dorsal
hook occasionally developed and a large fossa present for the
superior branch of the medial pterygoideus muscle.

Tables 4 and 5 list lower tooth measurements for specimens
referred to C. dirus.   Lower incisors are long and slender. I_1
differs from I^1 in having only a single labial basal cusp next to
the principal cusp. I_2 is similar to I_1, only considerably larger
and with a more prominent lingual cingulum. I_3 is slightly
larger than I_2, with a proportionally smaller basal labial cusp.
The canine is large and relatively broad at its base.

TABLE 5

Lower Tooth Dimensions of *Canis dirus*

	Dimension	N	O.R.	$\bar{X}$	S	C.V.
I_1	L	2	5.8 – 6.2	6.00	.282	4.700
	W	2	4.6 – 4.9	4.75	.212	4.463
I_2	L	2	7.2 – 7.6	7.40	.282	3.810
	W	2	6.2 – 6.4	6.30	.141	2.238
I_3	L	2	6.8 – 7.9	7.35	.777	10.571
	W	2	6.9 – 7.8	7.35	.636	8.653
C	L	8	13.5 – 14.7	14.07	.399	2.835
	W	8	10.2 – 11.7	11.01	.442	4.014
P_1	L	5	6.8 – 10.2	7.08	.370	5.220
	W	6	5.3 – 6.8	5.80	.558	9.620
P_2	L	8	12.7 – 14.8	13.52	.667	4.933
	W	8	6.4 – 8.1	7.03	.613	8.719
P_3	L	10	13.3 – 14.9	14.71	.780	5.302
	W	9	7.6 – 8.5	8.05	.324	4.024
P_4	L	14	17.2 – 19.4	18.09	.785	4.339
	W	16	9.2 – 11.5	10.01	.709	7.082
M_1	TrL	16	21.4 – 27.4	24.43	1.458	5.968
	TL	16	7.3 – 9.6	8.03	.615	7.652
	TrW	9	11.5 – 14.5	13.03	1.094	8.396
	TW	9	10.6 – 13.5	11.88	.866	7.238
M_2	TrL	2	7.6 – 7.7	7.65	.070	.915
	TL	2	4.0 – 4.1	4.05	.070	1.728
	TrW	2	8.9 – 9.0	8.95	.070	.782
	TW	2	7.1 – 7.4	7.25	.212	2.924
M_3	L	2	6.1 – 6.4	6.25	.212	3.392
	W	2	5.7 – 5.8	5.75	.070	1.217

P_1 is small, single-rooted, single-cusped, and ovoid in cross-section. The double-rooted P_2 has a posterior cusplet, varying in size from minute to large, developed between the principal cusp and the blunt heel of the tooth. The Bolivian specimen, MNHN TAR-751, lacks a posterior cusplet; however, a narrow wear ridge extends from the principal cusp to the heel of the tooth, perhaps obscuring this cusp (Fig. 13). Two posterior cusplets are behind the principal cusp on P_3. The first cusplet is much larger than the second and directly behind the principal cusp; the second cusplet always arises on the cingular heel. P_4 has two posterior cusplets behind the principal cusp, the second cusplet forming the cingular heel. M_1 is large relative to the other cheek teeth. The observed range (O.R.) of its maximum length ranges from 28.7 to 37.0 mm in the Talaran sample. The enamel surface of the tooth is coarsely crenulate. The metaconid is large and low. The talonid is relatively short and broad with a large hypoconid and smaller entoconid. Three minute posterior cusps are usually developed between the metaconid and entoconid (Figs. 8, 12). A metastylid is present at the base of the metaconid, and an entocristid is in an intermediate position between the metastylid and the entoconulid. The entoconulid is at the base of the entoconid. In specimens showing wear, the entoconulid and entocristid unite to form a single ridge, and only a metastylid and entoconid are distinguishable as cusps (e.g., see Fig. 13). A small, low hypoconular shelf is present posteriorly, and a transverse crest extends from this shelf to the metaconid. M_2 is relatively large and ovoid in cross-section, with a transversely wide trigonid and a short, narrow talonid. Mean trigonid width is 8.9 mm; talonid width averages 7.2 mm. An anterolabial cingulum borders the trigonid. A large hypoconid, smaller entoconid, and hypoconular shelf are present on the talonid. An entocristid and entoconulid, visible only on unworn specimens, are positioned between the metaconid and entoconid. M_3 is small, with an ovoid occlusal outline. A protoconid and slightly smaller metaconid and hypoconid are

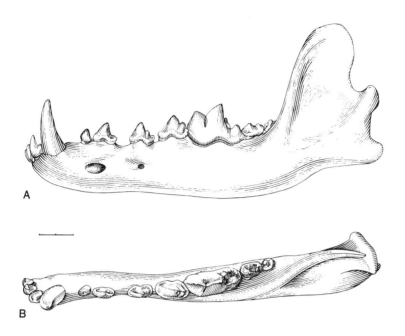

A

B

FIGURE 12. <u>Canis dirus</u> Leidy, 1858. ROM 2047, left mandible with complete dentition: (A) lateral and (B) occlusal views. Scale = 20 mm.

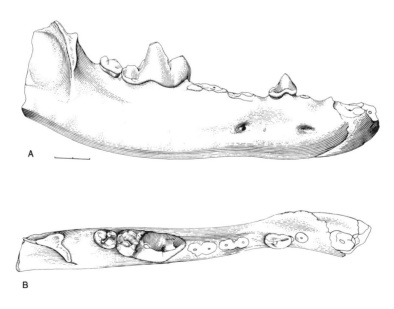

A

B

FIGURE 13. <u>Canis dirus</u> Leidy, 1858. MNHN TAR=751 (UCMP 123269), right mandible with P_2, M_{1-2}: (A) lateral and (B) occlusal views. Scale = 20 mm.

present.   A crest extends from the protoconid to the Anterolabial cingulum.

Remarks.   The long and involved nomenclatural history of C. dirus is summarized by Nowak (1979:107).   Following Nowak, I have not designated Aenocyon as a genus or subgenus, but have synonymized it under Canis.

   South American C. dirus are known from Lujanian-age deposits in Talara, Peru; Muaco, Venezuela; and Quebrada del Puente Alto, Bolivia.   The North American record of the dire wolf shows it more widely distributed, from Alberta to Mexico and from California to Florida, in Rancholabrean age deposits (Fig. 30).

   Churcher's (1959:564) referral of the Talaran large canid to C. dirus is based on comparison of the collection with figures and measurements of C. gezi, C. lupus furlongi (= C. milleri), C. nehringi, and C. dirus.   The data reveal that in nearly all dimensions the Talaran wolf falls closer to C. dirus than to the other species (Churcher, 1959:564, table 1).

   No significant cranial or dental differences were observed between the Rancholabrean and Talaran dire wolves.   A multivariate analysis of the postcrania of both suggests that the Talaran dire wolf, with its greater metapodial length, had longer feet than the Rancholabrean form (Kisko, 1967).   Aenocyon n.s. (?) which Royo y Gomez (1960:156) reported from Muaco, Venezuela, appears to be referable to C. dirus.   Unfortunately, the referred specimens have since disappeared from collections at the Universidad Central in Caracas (A. L. Bryan, pers. commun., 1977).   However, A. G. Edmond and C. S. Churcher of the Royal Ontario Museum studied this material prior to its disappearance, and their photographs (Plate 1) and measurements (Tables 2 and 5) compare favorably with both Talaran and Rancholabrean C. dirus.

   C. dirus is here regarded as the most derived species of the genus Canis in the New World.   The following combination of derived characters separates C. dirus from all other species of Canis: $P^2/_2$ with a posterior cusplet; P^3 with two posterior cusplets; M_1 with mestastylid, entocristid, entoconulid, and a transverse crest extending from the metaconid to the hypoconular shelf; M_2 with entocristid and entoconulid.

Canis gezi L. Kraglievich, 1928:45

(Figs. 14, 15; Plates 2, 3)

Stereocyon sp. Mercerat, 1917b:19.

Canis gezi L. Kraglievich, 1928:45, pls. 5-8; Rusconi,
    1931:14, 1936:202.

Macrocyon (Macrocyon) morenoi (?) Frenguelli, 1928:195,
    figs. 1-5.

Canis (Macrocyon) chapalmalensis Frenguelli, 1929:64.

Type. MACN 5120, a partially restored skull with right I^1, I^3, C, P^{2-4}, M^{1-2} (I^2, P^1 alveoli), and left I^3, C, P^{1-4}, M^{1-2} (I^{1-2} alveoli); associated mandible with a nearly complete dentition, right M_1 lacking a paraconid and right M_3 absent; associated postcranial elements, four cervical vertebrae, atlas and axis fragments, and left and right proximal humeral fragments.

Hypodigm. Type and MLP 52-IX-27-54, an incomplete left ramus with one-third of base of ascending portion and P_4 alveolus, M_{1-2}; MACN 10900, proximal part of left ulna; MLP 52-IX-27-68, left metatarsal III.

Stratigraphic and geographic distribution. The holotype was recovered from the "pampeano inferior," Ensenada Formation, excavation at Wilde Estacion, between the cities of Buenos Aires and La Plata, Buenos Aires Province, Argentina. MLP 52-IX-27-54 and MACN 10900 were collected from a region southwest of "Barranca Parodi," Miramar, Buenos Aires Province. MLP 52-IX-27-68 is from the base of cliffs between the mouth of Arroyo de las Brusquitas and Punte Vorohue, Miramar, Buenos Aires Province.

Age. Chapadmalalan (?) and Ensenadan.

Diagnosis. Supraoccipital shield with convex apex and no development of overhanging inion; wide palate; M^1 with a more anteriorly placed hypocone relative to the protocone; M^{1-2} with reduced labial cingula; P_3 single-cusped; P_4 with a single posterior cusplet.

Description.   L. Kraglievich (1928) described, measured, and figured specimens referable to C. gezi, and made brief comparisons with C. nehringi, C. dirus, and C. lupus. A supplemental description is included below and additional comparisons are made with a North American specimen referred to C. cf. C. dirus (Tedford and Taylor, pers. comm., 1978).

The skull of the holotype, MACN 5120, is incomplete, with the right frontal broken and portions of the alisphenoid, basisphenoid, basioccipital, and zygomatic portions of the squamosals missing (Pls. 2, and 3).   Some distortion of the cranium is apparent, particularly in the frontal region, which has been partly restored. Cranial dimensions, listed in Table 2, indicate that this is the smallest South American species of the genus. Skull width measured across the palate and cheek teeth, though smaller than in C. dirus and C. nehringi, suggests greater breadth relative to skull length.   The frontal sinus is large and penetrates the postorbital process, as shown by the inflated dorsal surface of the process. Posterior expansion of the sinus is suggested by lack of a sharp postorbital constriction. A prominent sagittal crest is developed.   The braincase is relatively large and dorsally inflated, measuring 38% of skull length.   Rostral length is 40% of skull length, slightly smaller than in C. dirus. The palate is relatively wide, measuring 18% of skull length.   The infraorbital foramen is positioned above the anterior root of P^3. Depth of the face is 19% of skull length, nearly equal to that of C. dirus. The jugal is also relatively large, its depth measuring 21.5 mm.   The supraoccipital shield is broad with a convex apex and no development of an overhanging inion (Pl. 3).   Tympanic bullae are relatively large and well inflated, measuring 29.4 mm in length. The foramen ovale and alisphenoid canal are joined in a single opening.

Upper cheek-tooth dimensions for MACN 5120 are listed in Table 4. Right I^1 and right and left I^3 are preserved. I^1 is small and transversely narrow with a worn subtriangular occlusal outline. The alveolus of I^2 suggests that this tooth was transversely narrow and slightly larger than I^1. I^3 is caniniform with a broad base. The canine is large and broad and shorter-crowned than in C. nehringi or C. dirus.

P^1 is single-rooted and single-cusped and anteroposteriorly shorter than in other South American Canis. P^2 is also single-cusped, but it is elongate and double-rooted with a prominent basal lingual cingulum. P^3 is obliquely oriented behind P^2 and has a posterior cusplet, behind which a prominent posterolingual cingulum is developed. P^4 is 32% longer than the combined length of M^{1-2}, and carries a small, well rounded, posterolingually directed protocone not well isolated from the body of the tooth. An incomplete basal lingual cingulum is posterior to the protocone.

A labial cingulum is developed only on the anterior and posterior ends of M^1. A small paraconule and larger metaconule are present, the metaconule being united to the protocone by a well worn crista (Fig. 14). A relatively large hypocone is in an anterolingual position relative to the protocone. A lingual cingulum extends from the paracone to the metaconule. M^2 is reduced in size, having a slightly larger paracone than metacone, a small protocone, and a relatively broad hypocone.

Both rami, lacking ascending portions, are associated with the skull in MACN 5120 (Fig. 15, Pl. 3). They are massive and deep, measuring 32.2 mm below M_1, and joined by a broad symphysis. The right ramus possesses three mental foramina positioned below the heel of P_1, the roots of P_2, and the anterior root of P_3.

Table 4 lists lower-tooth dimensions of MACN 5120 and MLP 52-IX-27-54. I_{1-3} increase progressively in size and transverse breadth at their bases. The canine is relatively short and broad,

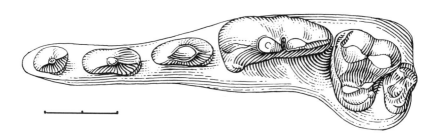

FIGURE 14. <u>Canis gezi</u> L. Kraglievich, 1928. MACN 5120 (UCMP 119292, type), left maxilla with P^{1-4}, M^{1-2}: occlusal view. Scale = 20 mm.

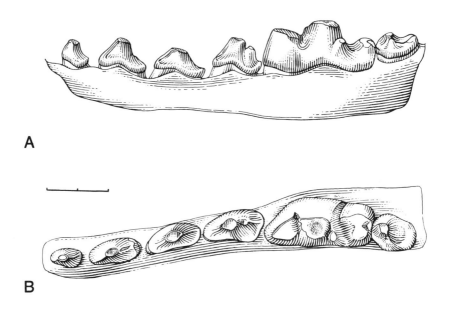

A

B

FIGURE 15. <u>Canis gezi</u> L. Kraglievich, 1928. MACN 5120 (UCMP 119292, type), right ramus with P_{1-4}, M_{1-2}: (A) lateral and (B) occlusal views. Scale = 20 mm.

approaching that of <u>C. dirus</u> in size. The right canine displays a prominent wear groove on its anterolingual surface. P_1 is single-rooted and single-cusped, terminating in a slightly upturned heel. P_2 is elongate, double-rooted, and single-cusped, a wear surface developed on the heel. Similar to P_2, P_3 is single-cusped as in its North American relatives $\underline{C}$. $\underline{armbrusteri}$ and $\underline{C}$. $\underline{falconeri}$. P_4 possesses a single posterior cusplet behind the principal cusp.

The M_1 trigonid is nearly twice as long as wide, with a well-worn paraconid-protoconid blade and a large metaconid. The talonid is nearly two-thirds as long as wide, with a large hypoconid and smaller entoconid. A small hypoconid is produced on a shelf between the entoconid and hypoconid. M_2 is reduced, having a large protoconid and a smaller metaconid on a transversely wide trigonid three-fourths as long as its width. The talonid is short, with a worn hypoconid and entoconid producing a flattened bench. Only the left M_3 is preserved, and it is small, single-rooted, and composed of one central cusp.

$\underline{Remarks}$. This species was established by L. Kraglievich (1928:45, pls. 5-8). It was named for professor W. Gez, a noted paleontologist in the province of Corrientes, Argentina. Earlier, Mercerat (1917b:19) referred MACN 5120 to $\underline{Stereocyon}$ sp. and noted its presumed affinity with $\underline{S}$. $\underline{nehringi}$ (= $\underline{Canis}$ $\underline{nehringi}$). L. Kraglievich (1928:45-50) differentiated $\underline{C}$. $\underline{gezi}$ from $\underline{C}$. $\underline{nehringi}$ and two large late Pleistocene North American canids - $\underline{C}$. (Aenocyon) $\underline{dirus}$ (= $\underline{C}$. $\underline{dirus}$) and $\underline{C}$. ($\underline{A}$.) $\underline{milleri}$ (= $\underline{C}$. $\underline{lupus}$ $\underline{furlongi}$).

Examination of fossil North American large canids suggests that $\underline{C}$. $\underline{gezi}$ is most similar to $\underline{C}$. cf. $\underline{C}$. $\underline{dirus}$ from the Irvingtonian of Nebraska (Tedford and Taylor, pers. comm., 1978). The following shared derived characters unite these species: broad palate (measured at P^1), M^{1-2} with reduced labial cingula, and a more anterior position of the hypocone relative to the protocone. $\underline{C}$. $\underline{gezi}$ can be differentiated from $\underline{C}$. cf. $\underline{C}$. $\underline{dirus}$ by its simpler $P^3/_3$ lacking posterior cusplets.

$\underline{C}$. (Macrocyon) $\underline{chapalmalensis}$ was founded by Frenguelli (1929:4) on the basis of an incomplete left ramus (MLP 52-IX-27-54) which he earlier (Frenguelli, 1928:195) suggested might be referable to $\underline{Macrocyon}$ ($\underline{Macrocyon}$) $\underline{morenoi}$ (= $\underline{Theriodictis}$ $\underline{platensis}$). A key character by which he diagnosed $\underline{C}$. ($\underline{M}$.) $\underline{chapalmalensis}$ was a convexity produced on the ventral border of the mandible that he referred to as a "subangular lobe." However, Frenguelli incorrectly evaluated this character. While C. (M.) chapalmalensis does exhibit a deep mandibular ramus which appears slightly convex relative to the base of the ascending ramus, this convexity is well within the range of variation seen in other species of Canis. A "subangular lobe" (sensu Huxley, 1880:251) is developed in Urocyon (North American Gray fox), Otocyon (Bat-eared fox), Cerdocyon (South American Crab-eating fox), Nyctereutes (Asian Raccoon dog), Speothos (South American Bush dog), and occasionally in the fossil canid Protocyon.

The fragmentary nature of the material does not permit recognition of a new species. I have followed L. Kraglievich (1929:253) in provisionally referring C. (M.) chapalmalensis to C. gezi on the basis of its deep, robust mandibular ramus (Table 2) and its broad lower molars.

According to Frenguelli (1929:65) the age of the deposit where the type and referred material of C. (M.) chapalmalensis were found is "Chapalmalense." L. Kraglievich (1928:56) pointed out, however, that this locality is a landslide deposit containing sediments ranging in age from "Chapalmalense" through "Ensenadense." Based on the preservation of the type and referred material, L. Kraglievich suggested that they were probably derived from sediments Ensenadan in age.

Canis nehringi (F. Ameghino, 1902:232)

(Figs. 16, 17; Plates 4, 5)

Canis (Chrysocyon) jubatus Burmeister, 1879:142, 217.

Canis jubatus fossilis Burmeister, 1885:95-107.

Palaecyon troglodytes(?) Nehring, 1885:109-122.

Dinocynops nehringi F. Ameghino, 1902:232, pls. 1-4.

Stereocyon nehringi Mercerat, 1917b:17.

Canis nehringi L. Kraglievich, 1928:41, pls. 1-4, 9.

Type. MACN 500, a nearly complete skull with left I^2, C, P^{1-4}, M^{1-2} (I^{2-3} alveoli), and right I^{1-2}, P^{1-3}, M^{1-2} (C, P^4 restored in plaster, I^3 alveolus); associated right ramus with P_{2-4}, M_{1-2} (C restored in plaster, P_1 broken at crown); right tibia.

Hypodigm. Type only.

Stratigraphic and geographic distribution. Type from "Pampean Formation," "pampeano superior" (fide Ameghino, 1902:232), Lujan, Buenos Aires Province, Argentina.

Age. Lujanian.

Diagnosis. Very similar to C. dirus in cranial and dental characters but with simpler construction of lower molars, lacking additional cusps and transverse crest linking hypoconid and metaconid; P_3 with posterior cusplet behind principal cusp.

Description. C. nehringi was previously described, measured, and figured by L. Kraglievich (1928) who made principal comparisons with C. dirus. A supplemental description is provided below.

The skull is complete except for the right maxilla, which has been partly restored in plaster (Pl. 4). Cranial dimensions are listed in Table 2. Greatest skull length measures 256.0 mm, slightly larger than in C. gezi. Skull width measured across the zygomatic arch is 78% of skull length. The frontal sinus is large and penetrates the inflated dorsal surface of the postorbital process. The sagittal crest, as in C. dirus, is uniformly high, strongly compressed, and accentuated by well defined temporal ridges, reflecting development of a large temporal muscle (Pl. 5). The braincase is relatively large, measuring 38% of skull length. The rostrum measures 43% of skull length, slightly larger than that of C. gezi. The relatively wide palate of C. nehringi measures 17% of skull length. An infraorbital foramen is positioned above the posterior root of P^3. Height of the skull from the outer alveolar margin of M^1 to the most ventral point of the orbit is 19% of skull length. The zygomatic arch is broadly

flared dorsoventrally.   Depth of the jugal measures 18.8 mm, the
smallest of any _Canis_ species described here, and suggests
development of a smaller masseter muscle.

The supraoccipital shield is narrow, lambdoidal crests
converging sharply at a triangular apex.   The inion projects
downward and backward beyond the condyles (Pl. 5), as in _C. dirus_.
Tympanic bullae are relatively large and inflated, measuring 29.2
mm long.   The foramen ovale and alisphenoid canal are separated by
a bony division into two distinct openings.

Table 4 lists the upper cheek tooth dimensions for MACN 500.
Right and left I^1 and left I^2 are preserved.   The first incisor is
small and transversely narrow with a subtriangular occlusal
outline. I^2 is similar to I^1 only larger.   The canine is large
and high-crowned, with a broad base.

P^{1-3} are similar to those of _C. dirus_ and _C. gezi_ and average
slightly smaller than in _C. dirus_. P^4 is 28% longer than the
combined length of M^{1-2}, and bears a small, rounded protocone and
a complete basal lingual cingulum posterior to the protocone.

A large paracone and smaller metacone are present on M^1.   The
labial cingulum is well developed (Fig. 16).   The trigon basin is
wide, and the protocone is well separated from the relatively
large metaconule and smaller paraconule.   Protocone and metaconule
are joined by a crista.   The hypocone is large and situated on a
wide shelf in a posterolingual position relative to the protocone
(Fig. 16).   An anterolingual cingulum extends from the paracone to
the metaconule. M^2 is reduced and narrow relative to its length
with a complete labial cingulum.   Paracone and metacone are low,
the paracone only slightly larger than the metacone.   The protocone is small, giving way to a hypocone shelf posterolingually.

The right ramus is associated with this skull, MACN 500.   It
is relatively narrow, short, and robust, with a single large
mental foramen below P_3.   Depth of the ramus below M_1 is 31.7mm;
its length is considerably shorter than mean values for _C. dirus_.
The angular process is expanded dorsoventrally, with a slight
dorsal hook and a large fossa for the superior branch of the

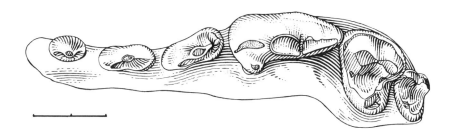

FIGURE 16. Canis nehringi (F. Ameghino, 1902).
MACN 500 (UCMP 119293, type), left maxillary with P^{1-4}, M^{1-2}:
occlusal view. Scale = 20 mm.

medial pterygoideus muscle.   The coronoid process is anteroposteriorly narrow and dorsoventrally high.

        Table 5 lists lower-tooth dimensions for MACN 500.   Lower
incisors and P_1 are not preserved, and the canine is completely
restored in plaster. P_2 is simple, double-rooted, and single-
cusped. P_3 is similar to P_2, but has a small posterior cusplet
behind the principal cusp; it is transversely broad, the posterior
half triangular in outline.

        M_1 is large and has a well developed paraconid-protoconid
blade. The trigonid is nearly twice as long as it is wide, with a
large, low-set metaconid. The talonid is short and broad, nearly
two-thirds as long as it is wide, with a well worn large hypoconid
and small entoconid (Fig. 17).   A small hypoconular shelf is
present. M_2 trigonid and talonid are transversely wide relative
to their respective lengths. An anterolabial cingulum is present.
The large protoconid is opposed by a smaller metaconid.   The
talonid is short and narrow with a large hypoconid. The entoconid
is broken away.   A small hypoconular shelf is produced behind the
hypoconid. M_3 is very reduced, with an oval occlusal outline, a
large protoconid, and a cingulum encircling the tooth.

Remarks.   Burmeister (1879:192, 217) suggested that MACN 500 is a
fossil specimen of an indigenous South American canid, the Maned
Wolf, Canis (Chrysocyon) jubatus (= Chrysocyon brachyurus).   In a

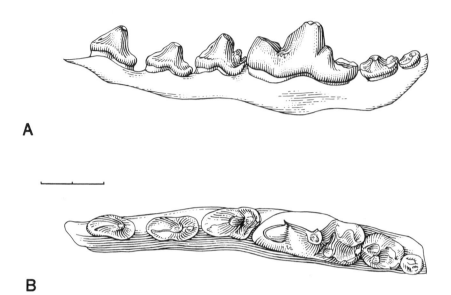

FIGURE 17. Canis nehringi (F. Ameghino, 1902). MACN 500 (UCMP 119293, type), right ramus with P^{2-4}, M_{1-2}: (A) lateral and (B) occlusal views.   Scale = 20 mm.

comparison of tooth dimensions of several species of Argentine canids, he illustrated the much larger size of MACN 500, referring it to Canis jubatus fossilis.   On the basis of MACN 500 (skull only), Ameghino (1902:232) established a new species within his newly founded genus - Dinocynops nehringi.   This same specimen, 15 years later, provided the basis for Mercerat's (1917b:17) proposed genus and species - Stereocyon nehringi.   L. Kraglievich (1928:41, pls. 1-4, 9) in a rediagnosis of MACN 500, referred it to the genus Canis and suggested that C. nehringi most closely compares with C. dirus.

     Nowak (1979:116) noted that these two species share the following characters: large size and massive proportions, broad frontal shield, prominent sagittal crest, narrow supraoccipital shield projecting far posteriorly, vertical plates of palatines flaring broadly anteriorly, postpalatine foramina opposite posterior ends of P^4, and relatively large carnassials. Synapomorphic characters uniting these two species include: narrow supraoccipital shield with triangular apex and overhanging inion, anterior lacerate and optic foramen set close together in common pit, and M^1 anterolingual cingulum seldom extending around the protocone.

Canis sp.

Macrocyon robustus F. Ameghino, 1881:306; 1889:307; 1898:194,
     196, fig. 60a-b; Revilliod, 1926:8.
Canis robustus L. Kraglievich, 1917:277; 1928:31; Revilliod,
     1926:8; J. L. Kraglievich, 1952:13n.
Felis sp., Mercerat, 1917a:11-12.

Material.   AMNH 11102, fragmentary right ramus with I_3, C in the crypt and dP_{3-4}; left maxillary fragment with P^1 alveolus and dP^3; left basicranial fragment (including posterior third of zygomatic branch of squamosal, auditory bulla, and portions of occipital and basisphenoid); parietal fragments; right jugal; anterior fragment of right scapula; right humerus.

Stratigraphic and geographic distribution.   "Pampean Formation" Arroyo Frias, near the city of Mercedes, Buenos Aires Province, Argentina.

Age.   Lujanian or Holocene (?).

Description.   The ramus is slender and deep,with two mental formina positioned below dP_3 and below the erupting C. I_3 is relatively large and spatulate with a small, lateral cusp on the basal cingulum.   Close behind I_3 is the relatively large C with longitudinal enamel ridges extending from the base of the crown to the sharp apex of the tooth.
     The small, double-rooted dP_3 has laterally compressed, high, sharp cusps.   Two posterior cusplets are positioned behind the

principal cusp, the second cusplet considerably smaller than the first. A well defined posterolingual cingulum arises behind the second cusplet. dP_4 is double-rooted, considerably larger than dP_3, and positioned close behind it. Both the trigonid and talonid of M_1 have high, sharp cusps. A small metaconid is present on the trigonid; the talonid has a prominent hypoconid and smaller entoconid. A small hypoconulid on the extreme posterolabial margin contributes to elongation of the tooth.

Remarks. The specific affinities of AMNH 11102 are not certain. It is a juvenile individual, and largely on the basis of size and dental similarities I have assigned it to Canis sp. The specimen smelled characteristically of burning organic matter when fired with a match, which suggests that it may be the unfossilized re-mains of C. familiaris. Comparisons of measurements of juvenile C. familiaris, C. dirus, and Protocyon troglodytes suggest that Canis sp. was a large animal, approaching C. dirus in size (Table 6).

Macrocyon robustus was founded on the basis of a humerus, tibia, and right P_4, material now lost (Ameghino, 1881:306). In an amended diagnosis, Ameghino (1889:307) selected a fragmentary right ramus as the type. He distinguished this genus from Canis on the basis of its larger size; shorter, more robust limbs; and large entepicondylar foramen in the humerus.

L. Kraglievich (1917:277; 1928:31) referred Macrocyon to Canis and noted that the specimen represented a very large individual. Cabrera (1932:31) considered C. robustus a juvenile C. nehringi, based on its similar size. However, the species name robustus had been preoccupied by Allen (1885:4) in his description of the domestic dog, C. (Pachycyon) robustus. J. L. Kraglievich (1952:13) reviewed the problem and reasoned that if one followed Cabrera's assessment, then C. ameghinoi would be the next available name to replace C. robustus Ameghino. However, he disagreed with Cabrera and retained both C. robustus and C. nehringi as valid species.

TABLE 6

Measurements of Mandibular Rami and Deciduous Lower Cheek Teeth

of Canis and Protocyon

Specimen	Depth of ramus below dp_4	dP_3 1	dP_4 1	TrL	TL
C. sp.					
AMNH 11102	27.5	8.8	16.0	9.5	6.3
C. familiaris					
UCMVZ 97600	14.4	---	12.4	7.6	3.6
UCMVZ 120938	10.2	6.1	10.0	6.6	3.5
C. dirus					
UCMP 13044	30.5	9.4	---	---	---
UCMP 28864	26.8	8.5	15.4	9.6	5.0
P. troglodytes					
UZM L6581	24.4	---	15.2	11.1	4.5
UZM L6579	22.5e	---	14.7	10.1	5.1

Theriodictis Mercerat, 1891:55

Dinocynops F. Ameghino, 1898:194 (partim).

Pleurocyon Mercerat, 1917a:13.

Canis (Theriodictis) L. Kraglievich, 1928:34.

Type specimens.   Theriodictis platensis Mercerat, 1891:55.
Dinocynops morenoi F. Ameghino, 1898:194.   Pleurocyon tarijensis
Mercerat, 1917a:13.

Geographic distribution. Argentina, Bolivia, and Ecuador.

Age. Ensenadan (middle Pleistocene) and Lujanian (late Pleistocene).

Type. Theriodictis platensis.

Included species. Type species and T. tarijensis.

Revised diagnosis. Frontal sinus large, penetrating postorbital process and extending posteriorly to the frontal-parietal suture (Fig. 9); deep zygomata with wide masseteric scar; long palatines extending beyond toothrow; wide palate; M^{1-2} with reduced hypocone; M^2 with reduced metacone; coronoid process anteroposteriorly broad and dorsoventrally low; angular process expanded dorsoventrally, with large fossa for inferior branch of medial pterygoideus muscle (Fig. 10A); M_1 lacking metaconid but possessing small entoconid; $M^2/_2$ small relative to $M^1/_1$; M_2 lacking anterolabial cingulum, with strong paracristid and relatively unreduced metaconid.

Theriodictis platensis Mercerat, 1891:55
(Figs. 18, 19; Plates 6, 7)

Theriodictis platensis Mercerat, 1891:55; 1917a:1; 1917b:17;
    Pascual et al., 1966:148, pl. 64.
Canis morenoi Lydekker, 1894:3-4, pl. 11, fig. la-b.
Dinocynops morenoi F. Ameghino, 1898:194, fig. 61; 1902:232;
    1906:401, fig. 267.
Palaeocyon platensis C. Ameghino, 1917:268.
Macrocyon platensis, L. Kraglievich, 1917:277, pl. 1,
    figs. d-e.
Macrocyon morenoi, L. Kraglievich, 1917:277, pl. 1, figs. a-c.
Palaeocyon troglodytes Revilliod, 1926:7, pl. 1, figs. 1-2,
    pl. 2, figs. 3-6.
Canis (Theriodictis) platensis, L. Kraglievich, 1928:34;
    Rusconi, 1931:14; 1936:202.

Canis (Macrocyon) morenoi, Frenguelli, 1929:63-69, figs. 1-3.

Canis? morenoi, Rusconi, 1929:4.

Holotype. MLP 10-80, left M_1 in ramal fragment.

Hypodigm.   Type and MLP 10-51, an incomplete skull missing pre-maxillae, with right C, P^{2-4}, M^{1-2} (P^1 alveolus), and left P^2, M^{1-2} (P^1 alveolus, anterior portion of P^3); associated right ramus with C, P_{2-3}, M_{1-3} (P_1 alveolus, posterior portion of P_4); MG 634/14, incomplete skull missing premaxillae, with right and left C, P^{1-4}, M^{1-2} (M^2 missing on right side), associated right and left rami with C, P_{3-4}, M_{1-2} (P_3 missing on right side); left lower C (Rusconi, 1929:4; Rusconi collection no. 208).

Stratigraphic and geographic distribution.   Holotype is from "pampeano inferior," "Pampean Formation," Mar del Plata, Buenos Aires Province, Argentina.   Type of Canis morenoi from "pampeano inferior," "Pampean Formation," collected near Central Estacion in the Capital Federal district of Buenos Aires.   MG 634/14 is from Punta Santa Elena, several feet above water level, on a river bank at the mouth of the Santa Elena River, north of Mar del Plata, Buenos Aires Province.   Left lower C from Olivos, left metatarsal from J. B. Anchorena, Buenos Aires Province.

Age.   Ensenadan and Lujanian.

Diagnosis.   Differs from T. tarijensis in having P^4 protocone medially directed, with a slight notch between the protocone and anterolabial tooth margin, and M^1 hypocone not as reduced.

Description.   L. Kraglievich (1928:34) briefly described MLP 10-80 and 10-51, and made comparisons with Protocyon troglodytes.   A re-description of T. platensis, including MG 634/14, is given below.

    The holotype, MLP 10-80, a nearly complete left M_1 in a ramal fragment, is missing only the enamel from the anterolabial surface

of the paraconid.   The lower carnassial is large with a high
paraconid-protoconid blade and a short, broad talonid.   No metaconid is present.   The broad talonid is worn nearly flat, and the
outline of a large hypoconid and a small entoconid are discern-
ible.   Depth of mandible below M_1 is 27.3 mm; M_1 length, 30 mm;
trigonid length, 20.9 mm; talonid length, 7.0 mm.

T. platensis is represented by two nearly complete skulls,
MLP 10-51 (Pls. 6 and 7) and MG 634/14.   Cranial dimensions of
these specimens are listed in Table 2.   The skull of MLP 10-51 is
missing the posterior portion of the parietals, zygomatic portions
of squamosals, lateral walls of temporals, and portions of
tympanic bullae, pterygoids, and basisphenoid.

Mean values for skull length average smaller than those for
South American fossil wolves (Canis).   In MLP 10-51, skull width
measured across the zygomatic arch is 55% of skull length.   Zygomata are deep with a wide masseteric scar.   Postorbital processes
are large and inflated.   The right postorbital process is broken
away, exposing the frontal sinus which, having penetrated this
process, extends posteriorly to the frontal-parietal suture, as
indicated by the degree of inflation of the lateral wall of the
braincase (Pl. 7).   The sagittal crest is prominent and strongly
compressed.   The braincase is relatively large and posteriorly
inflated; its width ranges between 30-32% of skull length. The
palate is wide and averages between 17-20% of skull length; this
dimension in C. gezi and C. nehringi ranges between 16-18%.   The
infraorbital foramen is above the posterior root of P^3.   T.
platensis has a relatively deep face; height of the skull from the
maxillary toothrow to the orbit measured an average of 16-20% of
skull length.   The supraoccipital shield is broad and rectangular;
its apex is convex and does not project beyond the condyles.
Tympanic bullae are relatively small and not strongly inflated;
they measure 22.1 mm in length in MLP 10-51.

Table 7 lists upper-tooth dimensions for specimens referred
to T. platensis.   None of the available material preserves I^{1-3} or
their alveoli.   The canine and P^{1-3} are shorter and narrower than

TABLE 7

Measurements of Cheek Teeth of Theriodictis

Upper

Dentition	C		P^1		P^2		P^3		P_4		M^1			M^2		
	L	W	L	W	L	W	L	W	L	W	L	W	TBL	L	W	TBL
T. platensis MLP 10-51	11.9	8.7	---	---	12.6	5.4	13.5	6.5	25.7	10.0	14.5	20.6	11.4	---	---	---
MG 634/14	14.9	9.1	7.4	5.4	13.8	6.0	14.9	---	28.4	11.5	---	16.3	---	6.6	12.2	---
T. tarijensis MACN 1452	---	---	---	---	---	---	---	---	26.4	12.0	14.4	---	11.3	---	---	---
T. cf. *T. tarijensis* MNHN, TAR 657	---	---	---	---	---	---	14.2	6.6	26.4	11.9	---	---	---	---	---	---

Lower

Dentition	P^2		P^3		P_4		M_1				M_2				M_3	
	L	W	L	W	L	W	TrL	TL	TrW	TW	TrL	TL	TrW	TW	L	W
T. platensis MLP 10-51	11.1	5.5	12.7	5.6	17.0	11.9	20.0	6.8	10.8	10.0	5.9	3.1	7.5	---	6.5	4.7
MG 634/14	---	---	---	---	15.9	7.6	22.5	8.5	11.6	---	---	---	7.5	---	---	---
Theriodictis tarijensis MACN 1452	---	---	---	---	29.1	15.3	23.1	7.3	---	---	---	---	---	---	---	---

those of South American <u>Canis</u>.   In MLP 10-51, P^3 is obliquely oriented behind P^2, and it is in direct anteroposterior alignment behind P^2 in MG 634/14. P^4 is large relative to M^{1-2}, with a small medially directed protocone.   A slight notch is developed between the protocone and the anterolabial tooth margin.   An incomplete basal lingual cingulum is developed posterior to the protocone. M^{1-2} have very reduced labial cingula, prominent only on the anterolabial tooth margin.   A relatively broad and narrow trigon basin supports a small metaconule and large protocone. The hypocone is positioned on a small shelf and in a posterolingual position relative to the protocone. M^2 is small relative to M^1, with a small metacone.   The hypocone shelf, although small, contributes to the posterolingual expansion of the tooth (Fig. 18).

Associated with the skull of MLP 10-51 is a right ramus missing only the incisor region (Pl. 7).   A nearly complete mandible is associated with the skull of MG 634/14.

The mandible is relatively long, 171.8 mm in MLP 10-51, the only specimen complete enough to permit measurement of this dimension. Depth of the ramus below M_1 ranges between 28.6 and 36.1 mm. A large mental foramen is positioned below P_{1-2}, and a smaller foramen is located below the anterior root of P_3.   The coronoid process is anteroposteriorly broad and dorsoventrally low. The angular process is greatly expanded dorsoventrally (Pl. 7),

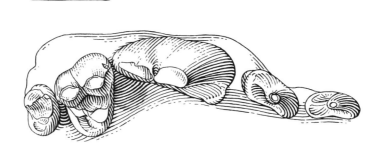

FIGURE 18. <u>Theriodictis platensis</u> Mercerat, 1891.
MLP 10-51   (UCMP 119321),   right maxillary with P^{2-4}, M^{1-2}:
occlusal view.   Scale = 20 mm.

and a large fossa is developed for the inferior branch of the medial pterygoideus muscle.

Lower cheek-tooth dimensions for specimens referred to T. platensis are listed in Table 7. Unfortunately, the only specimen which preserves a lower incisor is the right ramus of MG 634/14. I_3 is present in this specimen; however, it is extremely water-worn and is of little help in discerning the original size and morphology of the tooth. This same specimen preserves the canine, although extreme wear has again obscured morphology of the tooth. MLP 10-51 shows that this tooth is relatively large and transversely broad, although half of the crown, including the apex, is missing.

None of the available material has retained P_1. The only specimen preserving the P_1 alveolus is MLP 10-51. Judging from this specimen, the tooth was small, single-rooted, and ovoid in cross-section. P_2 is simple and single cusped; it is double-rooted, broadening slightly posteriorly, and terminates in a blunt heel. The anterior portion of P_4, including the principal cusp, is missing from MLP 10-51. The principal cusp in MG 634/14 is large and conical, although it has been worn level with the posterior cusplet. All of the available material shows development of two progressively smaller cusplets posterior to the principal cusp; the second cusplet forms the upturned heel of the tooth (Fig. 19).

M_1 is large relative to the other cheek teeth, with high, sharp cusps. The trigonid is nearly twice as long as wide. A metaconid is usually not developed, and I have interpreted its absence as the derived condition. However, as noted by L. Kraglievich (1928:37) and Revilliod (1926:4), the M_1 of MG 634/14 clearly shows development of a small, low metaconid. The rudimentary condition of this character in this specimen is interpreted as a trend toward loss. The talonid is short and broad, two-thirds as long as wide. A large well worn hypoconid and slightly worn small entoconid comprise the talonid. A small hypoconular shelf is present on MNHN GMT-1 and MLP 10-51. M_2 is reduced, with

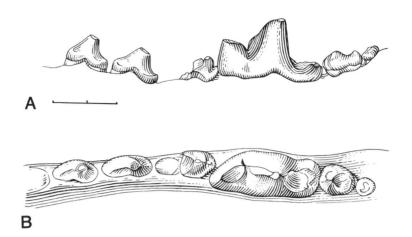

A

B

FIGURE 19. _Theriodictis platensis_ Mercerat, 1891. MLP 10-51
(UCMP 119321), right ramus with P_{2-4}, M_{1-3}: (A) lateral and (B)
occlusal views. Scale = 20 mm.

a transversely broad trigonid relative to its length and a talonid
more than twice as wide as long. The protoconid, although well
worn, is larger than the metaconid. The hypoconid and entoconid
are worn and form shelves rather than cusps (Fig. 19). M_3,
preserved in MLP 10-51, is small, with a circular crown and a
large central protoconid.

Remarks. MLP 10-80 provided the basis for Mercerat's (1891:51)
genus and species, T. platensis, which he attributed to the
creodont family Hyaenodontidae. The principal character Mercerat
used to demonstrate affinity between _Theriodictis_ and some
creodonts was the absence in both of the metaconid on M_1. As L.
Kraglievich (1917:264) noted, however, Mercerat's evaluation of
this character was erroneous, though _Theriodictis_ and some
creodonts (family Hyaenodontidae) share a few dental characters.
     F. Ameghino (1898:194) erected a new genus and species,
Dinocynops morenoi, on the basis of MLP 10-51, an incomplete skull
missing premaxillae and associated right ramus. Earlier, Lydekker
(1894:3) had referred this skull to Canis morenoi. Characters
that distinguish this taxon, according to F. Ameghino (1902:232)

are: short rostrum, elevated frontals, and a large, quadrate M^1 with well defined cusps.

L. Kraglievich (1928:35) referred both of these specimens to Canis (Theriodictis) platensis, the specific name platensis having priority over morenoi Lydekker (1894).   The fact that both specimens retained the entoconid made it necessary for Kraglievich to conserve the species platensis with the genus Canis.   Loss of the metaconid, however, permitted reference of these specimens to the subgenus Theriodictis.   Palaeocyon (= Protocyon) was differentiated from C. (T.) platensis by loss of the entoconid in the former. In this study, C. (T.) platensis has been removed from the genus Canis, and Theriodictis has been elevated to the generic level.

Revilliod (1924b:11; 1926:7, pls. 1 and 2, figs. 1-6) described MG 634/14, an incomplete skull and associated mandible, which he referred to Palaeocyon troglodytes.   Examination of a cast of this specimen reveals a number of similarities shared with the type of T. platensis, MLP 10-51, including frontal sinus development and type of angular and coronoid processes. Following L. Kraglievich (1928:32), this specimen is referred to T. platensis.

Lydekker (1894:3) reported that MLP 10-51 had been collected from lower deposits of the "Pampean Formation," "pampeano inferior."   Four years later, F. Ameghino (1898:194) indicated that this specimen had been collected from upper deposits of the "Pampean Formation," "pampeano superior" (piso Bonaerense). These two horizons of the "Pampean Formation" are usually interpreted as being Ensenadan and Lujanian in age, respectively.   In 1906, F. Ameghino altered his prior interpretation and concurred with Lydekker's original stratigraphic assignment for the specimen.

Theriodictis tarijensis (F. Ameghino, 1902:236)
(Plate 8)

Palaeocyon tarijensis F. Ameghino, 1902:232-236, pl. 1,
    figs. 2a-b, 3a-b; 1906:500; Trouessart, 1904:227;
    L. Kraglievich, 1917:273; Boule and Thevenin, 1920:233.

Pleurocyon tarijensis, Mercerat, 1917a:13.

Canis (*Theriodictis?*) *tarijensis*, L. Kraglievich, 1928:39.
Theriodictis tarijensis, Hoffstetter, 1963a:197.

Type. MACN 1452, a crushed skull with left C, P^{1-3} broken at crown, P^4, M^{1-2}, and right P^2 broken at crown, P^4-M^1; associated left ramus with P_4-M_1.

Hypodigm. Type only.

Stratigraphic and geographic distribution. The type is from Tarija, Bolivia.

Age. Late Ensenadan and/or early Lujanian.

Diagnosis. Differs from T. platensis in having P^4 protocone posterolingually directed, with strong notch between the protocone and anterolabial tooth margin, and M^1 with greater reduction of hypocone.

Description. T. tarijensis is represented by a single specimen, MACN 1452. Table 2 lists cranial measurements. The right side of the skull, from the parietal-temporal suture to the anterior part of the maxillae, has been crushed and deformed. Premaxillae and zygomata are missing. Deformation of the frontal region makes it difficult to evaluate the frontal sinus. However, it appears that the sinus was large and penetrated the postorbital process, although its posterior extension is impossible to ascertain. The sagittal crest is prominent, and width of the braincase measures 35% of skull length, slightly larger than in T. platensis. The rostrum is long relative to skull length, although this dimension could not accurately be determined. Palatal width at P^1 measures 17% of skull length. The infraorbital foramen is positioned above P^3. The inion does not project beyond the small, narrow supraoccipital shield. Tympanic bullae are relatively small and narrow, measuring 26.1 mm long.

Upper cheek-tooth dimensions for MACN 1452 are listed in Table 7. The upper incisors are missing, and P^{1-3} are broken at the crown. Judging from the alveoli, the upper premolars were long and narrow. P^3 is obliquely oriented behind P^2. P^4 is large relative to M^{1-2}, with a small protocone posterolingually directed. A well defined notch exists between the protocone and the anterolabial tooth margin (Pl. 8). The basal lingual cingulum, although present, is not continuous. M^{1-2} have reduced labial cingula, and a relatively broad trigon basin supports a small metaconule and large protocone. The hypocone forms a smaller, narrower shelf in comparison with T. platensis, and is in the posterolingual position relative to the protocone (Pl. 8). M^2 is small relative to M^1. Although the posterior portion of the tooth is missing, the hypocone shelf clearly contributed to posterolingual expansion of the tooth, as in T. platensis.

Associated with the holotype is a very fragmentary left ramus with P_4-M_1, neither tooth being complete (Pl. 8). The ramus is relatively deep, measuring 29.5 mm below M_1. The posterior portion of P_4 is broken; the alveolus indicates that the tooth was double-rooted, long, and narrow. M_1, positioned directly behind P_4, is missing the cusps of the trigonid. The talonid is short and triangular in outline, with a large, well developed hypoconid and a small entoconid positioned on the extreme lingual tooth margin (Pl. 8).

Remarks. MACN 1452, a crushed skull and fragmentary ramus, was collected on an expedition to Tarija, Bolivia, by the naturalist F. de Carles in 1888. This specimen was first described by F. Ameghino (1902:232-236), who figured the dentition and assigned the material to a new species, Palaeocyon tarijensis. L. Kraglievich (1928:29) referred this specimen to Canis; however, he questioned its assignment to the subgenus Theriodictis based on the fragmentary nature of the material. I have followed Hoffstetter (1963a:197) in referring this specimen to Theriodictis. It is difficult to separate T. tarijensis from T. platensis, owing to incompleteness of the material available. Several dental differences between these species are noted in the diagnosis.   The two species are also geographically separated with respect to their known records of occurrence.   A larger sample is necessary for further taxonomic refinement of Theriodictis species.

Theriodictis cf. T. tarijensis

Material.   MNHN TAR-657, right maxillary fragment with P^{3-4}.

Stratigraphic   and   geographic   distribution.   R.   Hoffstetter collected MNHN TAR-657 from Tarija, Bolivia.

Age.   Late Ensenadan and/or early Lujanian.

Description.   Table 7 lists tooth measurements for this specimen. P^3 is double-rooted and elongate, with a single principal cusp followed by a much smaller posterior cusplet. P^4 is relatively large, with a small rounded protocone in a posterolingual position.   A well defined notch is present between the protocone and anterolabial margin of the tooth.   An incomplete basal lingual cingulum is posterior to the protocone.

Remarks. This specimen most closely compares with T. tarijensis, but due to its fragmentary nature I have tentatively referred it to T. cf. T. tarijensis.   Both the type specimen MACN 1452 and MNHN TAR-657 share a similar degree of development in P^4 of the notch between the protocone and the anterolabial extremity of the tooth, and the posterolingual position of the protocone.

Theriodictis sp.
(Fig. 20)
Amphicyon argentinus F. Ameghino, 1904:122; 1906:402,
        fig. 269; 1909:423.
Canis argentinus L. Kraglievich, 1928:61; 1930:69.

Material. MACN 11611, an isolated right M^1; MACN 11606, an isolated left M^1; MNHN TAR-662, fragmentary left jugal with M^1.

Stratigraphic and geographic distribution. MACN 11611 is from "Hermososense horizon, Araucana Formation,"(?) Playa del Barco, Monte Hermoso, Buenos Aires Province, Argentina. MACN 11606 was collected along the Carcarana River near the bridge leading to the Rosario-Santa Fe highway, "Pampean Formation," Santa Fe Province, Argentina. R. Hoffstetter collected MNHN TAR-662 from Tarija, Bolivia.

Age. Montehermosan?, late Ensenadan, and/or early Lujanian.

Description. In comparison with Canis, the M^1 is relatively long and narrow, especially across the talon basin. The paracone and metacone are high, conical cusps. Labial cingula are very reduced, prominent only on the anterior margin of the paracone. A short crista unites the worn metaconule and small well rounded protocone. The hypocone forms a small shelf that is postero-lingually directed relative to the protocone (Fig. 20).

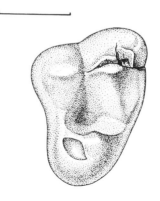

FIGURE 20. Theriodictis sp., MACN 11611 (UCMP 119291), right M^1: crown view.   Scale = 20 mm.

Measurements of M^1

	MACN 11611	MACN 11606	MNHN TAR-662
L	16.0 mm	14.8 mm	16.3 mm
TBL	12.1	10.5	11.5
W	23.1	22.5	22.4

Remarks. MACN 11611 (Fig. 20) was originally considered the type species of a new creodont (F. Ameghino, 1904:122), and later of a new species of Canis (L. Kraglievich, 1928:61). Referral of this specimen and of MACN 11606 and MNHN TAR-662 to Theriodictis is based on short talon basins relative to tooth widths and reduced hypocone shelves. The small sample of Theriodictis and the incompleteness of these specimens does not permit specific assignment. The M^1 of Theriodictis can be readily distinguished from Protocyon, which has a greatly reduced or absent hypocone shelf, and from Canis, which has a well developed hypocone on a broad shelf.

If the stratigraphic provenience of MACN 11611 is correctly reported, it represents the earliest known occurrence of the family Canidae in South America. However, according to Pascual (pers. commun., 1977), the locality where this specimen was collected contains sediments which range in age from Montehermosan through Lujanian. He suggested that, due to the uncertainty of its stratigraphic position within the section, it may be derived from sediments younger in age than Montehermosan.

Protocyon Giebel, 1855:851

Canis Lund, 1839-1842 (partim); Winge, 1895:26; Trouessart,
    1898:303 (non Linnaeus, 1758:32).
Palaeocyon Lund, 1843:78-79; F. Ameghino, 1889:310, 312;
    L. Kraglievich, 1928:27 (non Blainville, 1841:73-78).
Protocyon Giebel, 1855:851; Palmer, 1904:581; Simpson,
    1945:100; Paula Couto, 1946:66.
(?) Palaeospeothus Spillmann, 1941:197 (nomen nudum).

(?) <u>Palaeospeothos</u> Spillmann, 1942:380 (<u>nomen</u> <u>nudum</u>).

(?) <u>Palaeospeotus</u> Spillmann, 1948:261 (<u>nomen</u> <u>nudum</u>).

<u>Type</u>. <u>P</u>. <u>troglodytes</u>.

<u>Included species</u>. Type species and <u>P</u>. <u>orcesi</u> and <u>P</u>. <u>scagliarum</u>.

<u>Geographic distribution</u>. Argentina, Bolivia, Brazil, and Ecuador.

<u>Age</u>. Uquian (early Pleistocene), Lujanian (late Pleistocene) or Holocene (?).

<u>Revised diagnosis</u>. Frontal sinus large but not penetrating the postorbital process and extending posteriorly to the frontal-parietal suture (Fig. 9); deep zygomata with wide masseteric scar; long palatines extending beyond toothrow; wide palate; P^4 proto-cone very reduced; M^{1-2} with very reduced or absent hypocone; coronoid process anteroposteriorly broad and dorsoventrally low; angular process large, usually blunt without dorsal hook, fossa for inferior branch of medial pterygoideus muscle expanded (Fig. 10A); subangular lobe sometimes present; M_1 lacking metaconid and entoconid and possessing a basal cingulum lingual to the hypo-conid; $M^2/_2$ small relative to $M^1/_1$; M_2 lacking anterolabial cingu-lum and with strong paracristid and relatively unreduced metaconid.

<u>Remarks</u>. Simpson (1945:109) referred <u>Protocyon</u> to the subfamily Simocyoninae - a heterogenous group diagnosed on the basis of a trenchant talonid on M_1. In this group he included a number of fossil taxa and three living genera: <u>Speothos</u>, <u>Cuon</u>, and <u>Lycaon</u>. It has been noted by Hough (1948) and Thenius (1954) that the trenchant talonid developed independently several times in carnivore evolution, and that a taxonomic grouping at this level, on this basis, is not valid. Following Clutton-Brock, Corbet, and Hills (1976), I have not recognized the subfamily Simocyoninae and have placed the genus <u>Protocyon</u> within the subfamily Caninae.

The genus Protocyon was established by Giebel (1855:851) on the basis of a trechant talonid on M_1. In a footnote, Giebel explained the necessity for proposing a new genus for these species previously allocated by Lund (1843:50-54) to Palaeocyon. The problem was that the generic name Palaeocyon had been preoccupied by Blainville (1841:73, G. Suburus, pl. 13) in his description of P. primaevus, a member of the family Amphicyonidae.

A North American representative of the genus Protocyon has been reported as Canis texanus (Troxell, 1915:627) from Irvingtonian age deposits in Rock Creek, Brisco Co., Texas. The hypodigm consists of the type and paratypes (YPM 10058): incomplete left ramus with C, P^{1-4}, M^{1-2} (type); left M^1; left humerus; left anterior scapula fragment; left metatarsal IV; right cuneiform; and right pisiform. J. L. Kraglievich (1952:62) compared the North American material with Protocyon scagliarum and P. troglodytes and referred Troxell's species to the genus Protocyon. More recently, Nowak and Kortlucke (1984) assigned this material to Cuon on the basis of dental characters, and I have followed their assignment.

Separation of Protocyon from Cuon is based principally on morphology of the frontal sinus and angular process. Cuon, like Canis, illustrates the derived condition of the frontal sinus character. Both have a large frontal sinus which penetrates the postorbital process and extends posteriorly to the frontal-parietal suture. The frontal sinus in Protocyon is large but it does not penetrate the postorbital process. The angular process in Cuon, like Canis, has a large fossa for insertion of the superior branch of the medial pterygoideus muscle (Fig. 11). In Protocyon the angular process has the fossa for the inferior branch of this muscle expanded. Protocyon is further distinguished by retention of the metaconid on M_2 and loss of this cusp on M_1. The metaconid is absent from both M_{1-2} in Cuon.

Protocyon orcesi Hoffstetter, 1952:141

(Fig. 21)

(?) Palaeospeothos colomae Spillmann, 1942:380 (nomen nudum)

(?) Palaeospeotus colomae Spillmann, 1948:261 (nomen nudum).

Protocyon sp. Hoffstetter, 1949:8.

Protocyon orcesi Hoffstetter, 1952:141, pl. 4, figs. 26-37.

Holotype.   EPN V-2871, an incomplete left ramus with
C, P_2-M_2 (I_{2-3} alveoli).

Hypodigm.   Holotype, paratypes, and referred material.   Paratypes:
EPN V-2872, right fragmentary ramus with P_{1-4}, M_2; EPN V-2873,
right M_1; EPN V-2874, left M_1; EPN V-2877, left M^1; EPN V-2881,
right metacarpal V; EPN V-2883, fragmentary left metatarsal V.
Referred material: MNHN LAR-241 left M_1 (cast); MNHN LAR-242,
talonid portion of right M_1 (cast), fragmentary canine, posterior
portion M_1, fifth cervical vertebrae, lumbar vertebrae, caudal
vertebrae (2), metacarpal V (3), phalanx II.

Stratigraphic and geographic distribution.   Type, paratypes, and
referred material from La Carolina, Santa Elena peninsula,
Ecuador.

Age.   Lujanian (Carolinien).

Diagnosis.   Differs from P. scagliarum and P. troglodytes in
lacking M_3; differs from P. scagliarum in having overlapping
anterior lower premolars and in lacking an anterior cusplet on P_4.

Description.   P. orcesi was previously described, measured, and
figured by Hoffstetter (1952:141).   Brief comparisons were made by
him with P. troglodytes.   After examining casts of the holotypes
and several referred specimens, a supplementary description of
this species with an additional comparison to P. scagliarum is
provided.

The holotype, EPN V-2871, an incomplete left ramus, is relatively short, transversely broad, and deep, particularly below M_2. Hoffstetter's measurements of this specimen are listed in Table 8. Two small mental foramina are located below the anterior root of P_2 and below the small diastemata between P_2 and P_3. The angular process is large, with an expanded fossa for the superior branch of the medial pterygoideus muscle. The coronoid process is anteroposteriorly broad, although it tapers toward the dorsal margin. A marked convexity is present below M_2, which is interpreted as a weakly developed subangular lobe (Fig. 21). Unfortunately, the incisors are absent in the holotype. I_{2-3} alveoli suggest that these teeth were transversely narrow, I_3 being

TABLE 8

Lower Tooth Dimensions of Protocyon orcesi[1]

	Dimension	N	O.R.	$\bar{X}$	S	C.V.
C	L	1	14.5	---	---	---
	W	2	9.0			
P_1	L	2	6.6	6.6		
	W	2	4.6 - 4.7	4.65	.070	1.505
P_2	L	3	11.7 - 12.2	11.9	.265	2.218
	W	3	5.7 - 6.0	5.8	.173	2.982
P_3	L	2	14.0 - 14.5	14.25	.353	2.477
	W	2	6.5	6.5	---	---
P_4	L	2	15.4 - 16.0	15.7	.424	2.700
	W	2	7.0 - 7.4	7.2	.282	3.916
M_1	L	3	25.5 - 30.0	27.4	2.330	8.503
	TrW	3	10.0 - 11.4	10.5	.781	7.438
M_2	L	2	9.6 - 9.7	9.65	.070	.725
	TrW	2	7.3 - 7.4	7.35	.070	.952

[1]Measurements following Hoffstetter, 1952:143.

slightly larger. The canine is large, robust, and similar to that in $\underline{P.}$ $\underline{troglodytes}$.

P_1 is missing from the cast of the holotype and a small portion of the ramus is broken away, obliterating its alveolus. However, Hoffstetter (1952:143), in his description of the species, notes that this tooth is simple and single-rooted. The double-rooted, elongate, P_2 is single-cusped and terminates in a blunt heel. P_3 is so closely crowded behind P_2 that its antero-labial margin overlaps with the posterolingual margin of P_2 (Fig. 21). Its anteroposterior length is greater than P_2 and it possesses a minute posterior cusplet behind the principal cusp. Though transversely narrow, P_4 is posterolingually inflated, and the high principal cusp is followed by a sharp, small posterior

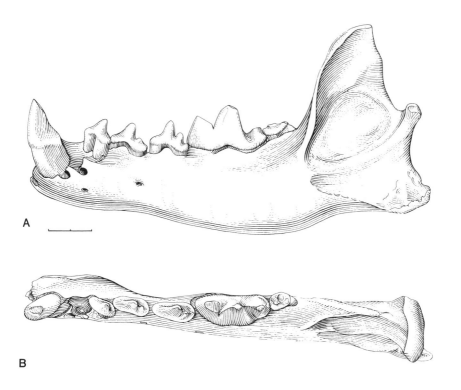

FIGURE 21. $\underline{Protocyon}$ $\underline{orcesi}$ Hoffstetter, 1952. EPN V 2871 (UCMP 123261, type), left ramus with C, P_{2-4}, M_{1-2}: (A) lateral and (B) occlusal views. Scale = 20 mm.

cusplet.   The posterior termination of this tooth is a slightly upturned heel.

Closely positioned behind P_4, the anterolabial margin of M_1 overlaps the posterolingual margin of P_4. M_1 is large and comparable in size to that in P. troglodytes. The slender trigonid is twice as long as it is wide. The metaconid is absent. However, Hoffstetter (1952:143) notes that one specimen, EPN V-2873, shows a slight outline of this cusp. The talonid is short and narrow with a single large, centrally positioned hypoconid opposed by a basal lingual cingulum (Fig. 21). M_2 is small relative to M_1, with a transversely broad trigonid and a short, narrow talonid. The paraconid and metaconid are low, the protoconid slightly larger. Cusps on the talonid of the holotype are worn nearly flat, and the crista obliqua connects the protoconid to the hypoconid. M_3 is absent in all of the available material referred to this species and was apparently not developed (Fig. 21).

Remarks.   As previously mentioned, Hoffstetter (1952) originally proposed and evaluated this species on the basis of material collected by F. Spillmann.   The species was named for G. Orces, a zoology professor at the University and Polytechnical School in Quito, Ecuador.

As noted by Hoffstetter, P. orcesi is similar to P. troglodytes, though more "specialized," and can be separated from the latter by the loss of M_3, interpreted as the derived condition.   P. orcesi and P. troglodytes share overlapping anterior lower premolars. Comparison of the cheek-tooth dimensions of P. orcesi (Table 8) with those of P. troglodytes (Table 11) indicates that P. orcesi is larger, having both longer and broader teeth.

Protocyon scagliarum J. L. Kraglievich, 1952:4
(Figs. 22, 23; Plates 9, 10)
Protocyon scagliarum J. L. Kraglievich, 1952:4-12, figs. 1-5,
7-9; Pascual et al., 1966, pl. 65, figs. a-c.

Type. MMP 164, skull with right C, P^{2-4}, M^{1-2} (I^3 broken at crown, P^1 alveolus), and left P^{2-4}, M^1 (I^{1-2} broken at crown, I^3 anterior half broken, C broken); associated mandible, right ramus with P_{1-4}, M_2 (M_1 trigonid broken), and left ramus with P_{3-4}, M_{2-3} (P_2 broken at crown, M_1 trigonid broken at crown).

Hypodigm. Type only.

Stratigraphic and geographic distribution. Type from Vorohue Formation, north-northeast of Mar del Plata in "barrancas littorales," near arroyo Santa Elena, Mar Chiquita, Buenos Aires Province, Argentina.

Age. Uquian.

Diagnosis. Differs from *P. orcesi* and *P. troglodytes* in having P_4 with anterior cusplet and lower premolars set off by diastemata; differs from *P. orcesi* in its smaller size; M_2 trigonid transversely broad, and M_3 present.

Description. *P. scagliarum* was previously described, measured, and figured by J. L. Kraglievich (1952). He made brief comparisons with *P. troglodytes* and *Speothos*. A supplemental description is provided below. Cranial measurements are listed in Table 2.

The skull of MMP 164 is nearly complete, missing only the premaxillae (Pl. 9). It is relatively short with broad proportions, its greatest length measuring only 214 mm. Skull width measured across the zygomatic arch is 74% of skull length. Zygomata are relatively deep with a wide masseteric scar. The postorbital processes are short. Judging from the depressed dorsal surface of the process, the frontal sinus, though large, does not penetrate the process (Pl. 9). The sagittal crest is low, and temporal ridges are weakly developed. Were it not for the relatively large braincase, the low sagittal crest might suggest development of a small temporal muscle. Width of the braincase, however, measures 35% of skull length and provides the needed surface area for a large temporal muscle. A 1 cm perforation on the left parietal was interpreted by J. L. Kraglievich (1952) to be the result of a blow inflicted by the canine of a predator. A characteristic feature of this genus is its shortened rostrum relative to that of Canis and Theriodictis. This dimension measures 38% of skull length. The palate is moderately wide, measuring 16% of skull length. Palatines are long, extending slightly beyond the toothrow (Pl. 9). The infraorbital foramen is above the posterior root of P^3. P. scagliarum has a relatively deep face, suggested by skull height from the maxillary toothrow to the orbit, which measures 17% of skull length. The zygomata are well arched dorsoventrally. Depth of the jugal measures 15.3 mm. The supraoccipital shield is small but relatively broad, with a convex, flattened apex. Tympanic bullae are relatively large and well inflated, with an external auditory meatus of large diameter.

I^{1-2} are broken at the crown. Their alveoli are small and transversely narrow. The I^3 is caniniform and proportionally much larger than I^2, with a strong posteromedial cingulum. The canines are relatively short and robust and slightly smaller than those of P. troglodytes.

Dimensions of the upper cheek teeth are listed in Table 9. Upper and lower premolars and molars have high, sharp cusps displaying little wear. P^1 is missing, though the alveolus indicates that the tooth was small. P^2 has a single posterior cusplet behind the principal cusp. The tooth is transversely broad and terminates in a slightly rounded heel. P^3 obliquely oriented behind P^2, is larger than P^2 but with the same principal cusp and accessory cusplet morphology. P^4 is 18% longer than the combined lengths of M^{1-2}, and has a very small, anteriorly directed protocone that is not well separated from the rest of the tooth. An incomplete basal lingual cingulum is present posterior to the protocone.

M^1 has a reduced labial cingulum developed only on the anterior end of the paracone (Fig. 22). Paracone and metacone are sharp and conical. The trigon basin is narrow, flanked by a small metaconule and paraconule. The protocone is only slightly smaller than the metacone. An anterior cingulum extends from the paracone lingually around the protocone to the metaconule. The hypocone is absent and in its place is a narrow ridge (Fig. 22). M^2 is very

TABLE 9

Upper and Lower Teeth of _Protocyon_ scagliarum,
Holotype MMP 164

C	11.5	7.9
P^1	---	---
P^2	11.2	5.4
P^3	13.0	6.0
P^4	25.0	---
M^1	14.7	19.6
M^2	6.4	8.6
C	---	---
P_1	6.0	4.6
P_2	10.0	5.6
P_3	12.2	5.7
P_4	14.6	6.9
M_1	17.5e (TrL)	9.9 (TrW)
	6.5 (TL)	9.1 (TW)
M_2	5.6 (TrL)	8.5 (TW)
	3.9 (TL)	6.2 (TrW)
M_3	4.2	4.4

reduced relative to M^1, with a large, conical paracone, a minute metacone, and a small protocone.

Associated with the skull are incomplete right and left rami missing their anterior portions. The rami are short and robust; their depth below M_1 measures 28.0 mm. A small mental foramen is below the anterior root of P_3. A large blunt angular process has an expanded fossa for the inferior branch of the medial pterygoideus muscle. The coronoid process is anteroposteriorly broad and dorsoventrally low. A subangular lobe is weakly developed (Pl. 10).

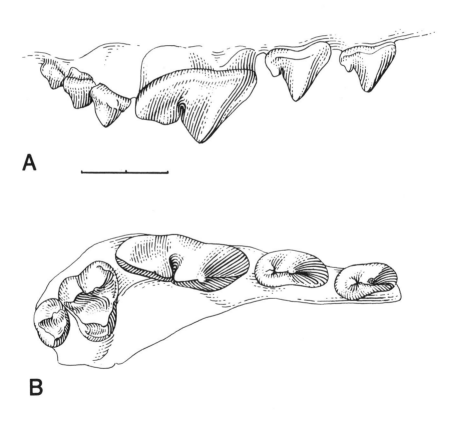

FIGURE 22. <u>Protocyon</u> <u>scagliarum</u> J. L. Kraglievich, 1952. MMP 164 (UCMP 119311, type), right maxillary with P^{2-4}, M^{1-2}: (A) lateral and (B) occlusal views. Scale = 20 mm.

Lower tooth measurements are also listed in Table 9. P_1 is single-rooted and small with a high, single cusp having an ovoid cross-section. The double-rooted P_2 has a single, piercing cusp. Behind the principal cusp on P_3 is a small posterior cusplet. P_4 has a minute basal anterior cusplet in front of the principal cusp only on the left ramus (Fig. 23). A large broad posterior cusplet is behind the principal cusp.

M_1 lacks a metaconid. The talonid is short and has a large, conical-crested hypoconid. Lingual to the hypoconid is a basal cingulum (Fig. 23). M_2 is relatively large, with a transversely broad trigonid and a strong paracristid. The protoconid is larger than the metaconid, and the crista obliqua connects this cusp to the hypoconid. M_3 is very reduced, single-rooted, and circular, with a single central cusp.

Remarks. <u>P</u>. <u>scagliarum</u> was established by J. L. Kraglievich (1952:4) on the basis of MMP 164, a skull and mandibles. The specimen was collected by Lorenzo and Galileo Scaglia in May 1944, and it is the earliest well documented occurrence of the family Canidae in South America.

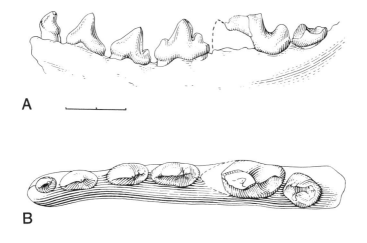

FIGURE 23. <u>Protocyon scagliarum</u> J. L. Kraglievich, 1952. MMP 164 (UCMP 119311, type), right ramus with P_{1-4}, M_{1-2}: (A) lingual and (B) occlusal views. Scale = 20 mm.

J. L. Kraglievich (1952:17) drew comparisons between P. scagliarum and the extant bush dog Speothos venaticus, suggesting that both genera were derived from a common ancestor. While they are superficially similar in having shortened crania and rostra, the following characters distinguish Protocyon from Speothos: (1) large frontal sinus which does not penetrate postorbital process; (2) premolars that are short and high-crowned; and (3) P_4 with an anterior cusplet occasionally developed. P. scagliarum can be separated from P. troglodytes and P. orcesi using a single character, P_4 with an anterior cusplet. This derived character is also shared among several species of Cuon from North America and Europe (Nowak and Kortlucke, 1984).

Protocyon troglodytes (Lund, 1839b:223)

(Fig. 24; Plate 11)

Canis lycodes Lund, 1843:81, pl. 45, fig. 3; Gervais and
    Ameghino, 1880:40; F. Ameghino, 1889:305, 1898:192.

Canis troglodytes Lund, 1839b:223; 1840a:14, pl. 18, fig. 7;
    1840b:312; 1842:62; 1843:47; Blainville, 1843:130;
    F. Ameghino, 1889:315; Winge, 1895:16, 26-28, pl. 2,
    figs. 1-4, pl. 3, figs. 1-8; Gervais and Ameghino,
    1880:34.

Canis spelaeus Gervais and Ameghino, 1880:34.

Canis musculosus F. Ameghino, 1882:38; 1889:305.

Palaeocyon troglodytes Lund, 1843:50-54, pl. 44, figs. 1-12,
    pl. 45, figs. 1-2; Gervais and Ameghino, 1880:34;
    L. Kraglievich, 1928:27.

Protocyon troglodytes Giebel, 1855:851; J. L. Kraglievich,
    1952:54.

Co-types of P. troglodytes. UZM L:228, left P^4; 187, right maxillary fragment with P^4-M^1; 240, canine; 236, incomplete right ramus with C, P_1 (broken at crown, P_2 anterior half broken), P_3, M_1; 251, left M^2; 249, right I_3; 248, left I_3; 257, I_2.

Hypodigm. Co-types and in UZM L:250, fragmentary M_1; 237, right ramus with M_1; 5697 and 5698, incomplete right maxillary with I^3, C, P^{1-4}, M^1; 5700, incomplete right ramus with M_{1-3}; 5699, incomplete left maxillary with C, P^{1-2}, P^4 (P^3 alveolus); 643, left maxillary fragment with P^4; 2145, right P^4; 2146, fragmentary left P^4; 2157, left ramal fragment with C, P_{2-4}; 6582, right maxillary fragment with dP^{3-4}; 12620, right M_2; 301, right fragmentary ramus with P_{2-3} (broken at crown), M_1 (P_4 alveolus); 246, left P_2, C; 234, left ramal fragment with P_{1-3}; 249, right I_3; 244, C; 238, right P^1; 254, I_1; 245, C, 10709, fragmentary right ramus with M_1 in crypt; 6716, fragmentary left mandible with C, P_1, M_1 in crypt; 6581 and 6579, fragmentary right rami with C, dP_1, dP_4, P_4, M_1; 10708, occipital; 5756, proximal two-thirds of right ulna; 7405, proximal right ulna; 772, 1043, proximal left ulna; 762, proximal end left ulna; 764, distal end of articulated left radius and ulna; 765, distal and proximal ends of radius; 12416, distal left radius; 769, 2163, distal right humerus; 54, proximal right humerus; 761 proximal end left humerus; 1067, 1068, ulna; 1050, metacarpal IV; 1059, scapholunar; 1009, magnum; 12377, 12402, 3747, metacarpal V; 4736, proximal left femur; 770, distal femur; 775, proximal left tibia; 8088, distal right tibia; 769, 775, shafts of tibiae; 1537, 56, 776, calcanei; 53, L57, L10710, astragali; 89, 108, 1061, cuboid; 1063, 1062, 29, 1538, navicular; 1064, 1065, pisiform; 108, 1066, metatarsal II; 117, 397, metatarsal III, 393, 60, 12388, right metatarsal IV; 8565, 4737, metatarsal V; 1124, fragmentary metapodial; 9335, 12412, distal metapodial; 12403, 10716, 10719, 10718, 12405, 12404, 267, metapodials; 10717 proximal metapodial; 10720, phalanges; ?, axis; 5693 axis; ?, 8068, 400, 46, 3746, cervical vertebrae; 10714, 10715, 10711, vertebrae; 12346, 12347, 12348, caudal vertebrae; 1085, 1088, 1092, 1-86, 1083, 1082, 1091, 1090, 1084, 1089, 1087, sternumbrae; 5748, 5747, innominate; MNHN NUA-91, fragment of left ramus with M_{1-2} (M_3 alvolus). UF 27889, fragmentary ramus with posterior half P_4, M_1 (M_2 alveolus); UF 26911, left maxillary fragment with P^3 and anterior portion of P^4;

associated right and left rami with C, P_{1-4} (broken at crown),
M_{1-3}; MNHN NUA-91, fragmentary left ramus with M_{1-2} (M_3
alveolus).

Stratigraphic and geographic distribution. - Types and referred
UZM L material were all collected from the Lagoa Santa Caves,
Minas Geraes, Brazil, by P. W. Lund; their specific collection
sites are as follows: Lapa de Periperi (dos Indios no. 1): UZM
L:27, 29, 46, 53, 54, 56, 57, 60, 62, 84, 108, 117, 187, 234, 236,
238, 240, 244, 245, 246, 248, 249, 250, 251 254, 267, 301, 393,
397, 399, 400, 761, 764, 765, 768, 769, 770, 775, 776, 1061, 1062,
1063, 1066, 1082, 1083, 1084, 1085, 1086, 1087, 1088, 1089, 1090,
1091, 1092, 1050, 1059, 1064, 1065, 1067, 1068, 1069, 1108, 4736,
4737, 8565, 12346, 12347, 12348, 12620; Lapa dos Porcos: UZM
L:643; Lapa da Escrivania no. 5: UZM L:5693, 5696, 5697, 5698,
5699, 5700, 5756, 7405, 8068, 8088, 12412; Lapa da Escrivania no.
11: UZM L:6511, 6579, 6581, 6582, 6719, 10708, 10709, 10710,
10711, 10714, 10715, 10716, 10717, 10718, 10719, 10720, 12388,
12402, 12403, 12404, 12405; Lapa da Lagos do Sumidouro: UZM
L:2145, 2146; Lapa dos Tatus: UZM L:2157; Lapa dos Fatus: UZM
L:2163, 9335, 12377, 12416; Lapa do Cavallo: UZM L:772; Lapa do
Bahu: UZM L:1537. UF 26911, 27889, Tarija, Bolivia; MNHN NUA-91,
Nuapua, Bolivia.

Age. Lujanian and Holocene.

Diagnosis. Differs from P. orcesi in having M_3 present and M_2
trigonid transversely broad; differs from P. scagliarum in lacking
an anterior cusplet on P_4 and overlapping lower premolars.

Description. Thirty-three fragments of maxillae, mandibles, and
isolated teeth collected from the Lagoa Santa Caves in Brazil have
been used in this composite description. The association of
isolated teeth with this species is based upon size, morphology,
and locality provenience.

Among maxillae fragments, only UZM L5697 permits mensuration. Depth of its jugal measures 20.0 mm, which is nearly equal to that of $\underline{C}$. $\underline{dirus}$, suggesting development of a large masseter muscle in this species.   The infraorbital canal in this specimen is above P^3.

Measurements and statistics for upper teeth are listed in Table 10.   Only I^3 has been found in association with other cheek teeth.   This tooth is caniniform with a strong posteromedial cingulum (Fig. 24).   A prominent narrow wear surface extends from

TABLE 10

Upper Tooth Dimensions of $\underline{Protocyon}$ $\underline{troglodytes}$ from Brazil

Dimension		N	O.R.	$\bar{X}$	S	C.V.
I^3	L	1	8.6	---	---	---
	W	1	7.0	---	---	---
C	L	2	12.2 - 12.5	12.35	.212	1.716
	W	2	8.1 - 8.4	8.25	.212	2.569
P^1	L	2	7.0 - 7.1	7.05	.070	.992
	W	2	5.3 - 5.6	5.45	.212	3.889
P^2	L	1	12.3	---	---	---
	W	2	5.5	5.50	---	---
P^3	L	1	13.4	---	---	---
	W	1	6.5	---	---	---
P^4	L	6	25.8 - 27.9	26.91	.919	3.415
	W	6	12.1 - 13.7	12.55	.615	4.900
M^1	L	2	14.6 - 16.2	15.40	1.131	7.344
	W	2	20.3 - 20.6	20.45	.212	1.036
M^2	L	1	7.3	---	---	---
	W	1	11.1	---	---	---

the base of the crown to the apex of the tooth.   The canine is short and robust. The anterior premolars are well spaced in the toothrow.   The first premolar is single-rooted and single-cusped. The double-rooted P^2 has a transversely broad crown consisting of transversely broad crown consisting of a large, high principal cusp followed by a sharp posterior cusp. Posterior termination of the tooth is in a blunt heel. P^3 is similar in morphology to P^2, with a greater anteroposterior length.   Its position in the toothrow, as shown in UZM L5697, is slightly oblique relative to P^2. P^4 is large relative to the other cheek teeth, with a low-crowned paracone-metacone blade.   The small, low, rounded protocone is posterolingually directed (Fig. 24). Most specimens do   not   show   any   notching   between   the   protocone   and   the anterolabial extremity of the tooth; UZM L:187 and 228 are

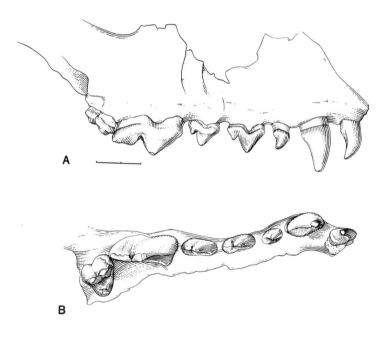

A

B

FIGURE 24. Protocyon troglodytes (Lund, 1839b). UZM L5697, L5698 (UCMP 123384),   right   maxillary   with I^3, C, P^{1-4}, M^1: (A) lateral and (B) occlusal views. Scale = 20 mm.

exceptions and show pronounced notching. UZM L187 and 2145 show development of a slight lingual cingulum posteriorly. A labial cingulum is on the anterior end of the paracone and to a lesser degree on the posterior margin of the metacone of M^1. The piercing protocone is prominent, its lingual margin giving way to a relatively steeply sloped hypoconal ledge, in a posterolingual position relative to the protocone (Fig. 24). On a single specimen, UZM L187, the anterolingual cingulum can be traced circling the protocone. None of the maxillae found have preserved the M^2 in association with other cheek teeth. An isolated left M^2, UZM L251, is the only available specimen. It is double-rooted, lacks a labial cingulum, and consists of a low and relatively small protocone. The hypocone is low, narrow, and in a posterolingual position relative to the protocone.

UZM L236, an incomplete right ramus, has two mental foramina present below P_1 and beneath the anterior root of P_2. In this specimen the ramus appears relatively deep, though measurement was not possible due to its incompleteness. Unfortunately, none of the referred material has the angular process preserved.

Measurements and statistics for lower teeth are listed in Table 11. Only isolated lower incisors have been recovered. The only available specimen of I_1, UZM L254, is transversely narrow with a single cusp. I_2, represented by UZM L257, is slightly larger and displays a lateral cusplet; the crown is worn to the same height as the cusplet. Two specimens are referable to I_3, UZM L:248 and 249. They are caniniform, subtriangular in outline, and display lingually prominent narrow, elliptical wear grooves extending from the medial portion of the tooth to the base of the crown. A lower canine was found in association with other cheek teeth in UZM L2157, left ramal fragment with C, P_{2-4} (Pl. 11). The tooth is relatively large, with a broad base and a lingual wear groove similar to that displayed by I_3.

The only available specimen of P_1 is in a left ramal fragment with P_{1-3}, UMZ L234. The tooth is small, single-rooted, single-cusped, and lateromedially broad. The double-rooted,

TABLE 11

Upper Tooth Dimensions of Protocyon troglodytes from Brazil

Dimension		N	O.R.	X̄	S	C.V.
C	L	1	12.5	---	---	---
	W	1	9.3	---	---	---
P$_2$	L	3	6.9 − 11.6	9.86	2.581	26.176
	W	3	5.1 − 6.1	5.53	.513	9.276
P$_3$	L	2	12.7 − 13.0	12.85	.212	1.649
	W	2	5.6 − 5.8	5.70	.141	2.473
P$_4$	L	2	14.5 − 15.3	14.90	.565	3.791
	W	2	6.5 − 6.6	6.55	.070	1.068
M$_1$	TrL	5	19.3 − 23.0	21.22	1.657	7.808
	TL	4	6.6 − 7.6	7.00	.432	6.171
	TrW	4	9.8 − 11.7	10.52	.095	.903
M$_2$	TrL	2	4.7 − 6.3	5.50	1.131	20.563
	TL	2	3.4 − 3.8	4.05	.919	22.691
	TrW	2	7.0 − 8.6	7.80	1.131	14.500
M$_3$	L	2	4.7 − 5.3	5.00	.424	8.480
	W	2	4.4 − 4.8	4.60	.282	6.130

posterolingually broad P$_2$ consists of a single worn principal cusp in UZM L2157. The other available specimen, UZM L234, shows development of a minute posterior cusplet behind the principal cusp. P$_3$ is similar to P$_2$, with a greater anteroposterior length and variable development of a posterior cusplet behind the principal cusp. In an unnumbered UZM L specimen, P$_3$ lacks a posterior cusplet, whereas UZM L2157 has a relatively large, piercing cusplet present behind the principal cusp (Pl. 11). This tooth terminates abruptly in a blunt heel. P$_4$ is larger than P$_3$, with a greater transverse breadth posteriorly. A posterior cusplet, relatively larger than in P_3, is always present behind the principal cusp. This tooth is elongated beyond the posterior cusplet terminating in an upturned sharp heel.

M_1 is large relative to the other cheek teeth. The trigonid is twice as long as it is wide, with a high paraconid-protoconid blade. No metaconid is present. The short, narrow talonid displays a prominent lingual cingular shelf opposite the large conical hypoconid (Pl. 11). M_2 has a relatively large transversely broad trigonid with low conical protoconid and smaller metaconid. A strong paracristid is usually developed (Pl. 11). The talonid is short and wide, with cusps worn nearly level with the crown; a ridge connects the protoconid and hypoconid. M_3 is a very reduced, single-rooted tooth with an ovoid occlusal outline. This tooth, represented by UZM L:5700, bears a large protoconid and a strong paracristid.

Deciduous dentitions referred to P. troglodytes have been recovered from the Lagoa Santa Caves. The deciduous upper dentition is represented by UZM L6582, right maxillary fragment with dP^3-dP^4. Table 12 lists upper-tooth measurements of this specimen and of C. dirus and C. familiaris. An effort was made to compare measurements from specimens showing the same stage of tooth eruption.

dP^3 is long relative to dP^4, with a high paracone-metacone blade and a very small posterolingually directed protocone. Positioned next to it is the molariform dP^4. The paracone and slightly smaller metacone are high, sharp cusps. The talon basin is narrow, with a small protocone arising on the posterolingual cingulum. The posterolingual portion of the tooth forms a rounded, shallow basin.

The deciduous lower dentition is represented by UZM L:6581, and 6579, fragmentary right rami with C, dP_1, dP_4, P_4, M_1, and UZM L7616, fragmentary left ramus with C, P_1, M_1, in crypt. dP_2 is diminutive and double-rooted. The principal cusp is sharp, and its posterior portion strongly sloped relative to the base of the crown. Only the alveolus of dP_3 is present. It suggests that the

TABLE 12

Measurements of Upper Deciduous Cheek Teeth of
Protocyon troglodytes, Canis dirus, and C. familiaris

| | dP^3 | | dP^4 | |
	L	W	L	W
P. troglodytes				
UZM L6582	15.5	5.3	9.8	12.1
C. dirus				
UCMP 123229	11.2	6.2	9.1	10.7
UCMP 12300	10.7	5.8	8.0	9.3
C. familiaris				
UCMVZ 120939	9.2	3.4	7.0	8.3

tooth was double-rooted, the posterior root being larger. dP_4 has a well developed carnassial blade with a small metaconid present. The short talonid displays a large, high hypoconid. From the stage of eruption of M_1 in its crypt, a large hypoconid is present with no development of a metaconid.

Referred material. Also referred to this species is MNHN NUA-91, a fragmentary left ramus with M_{1-2} (M_3 alveolus) from Nuapua, Bolivia; MNHN GMT-1, incomplete left ramus with P_{2-3}, M_{1-2}, from Guamote, Ecuador; UF 27889, a fragmentary left ramus with posterior half P_4, M_1 (M_2 alveolus); and UF 26911, left maxillary fragment with P^3 and anterior portion of P^4, and associated right and left rami with C, P_{1-4} (broken at crown), and M_{1-3}, from Tarija, Bolivia.

In UF 26911, P^3 is very small relative to P^4 and consists of a high-crowned single principal cusp. The protocone on P^4 is small and posterolingually directed. Table 13 lists comparative tooth dimensions for these specimens.

MNHN NUA-91 preserves the posterior third of the horizontal ramus and most of the ascending ramus, though the toothrow has been crushed. The ramus is robust and deep, measuring 33.1 mm below M_1. The Tarijan and Ecuadorian specimens are shallower in

TABLE 13

Measurements of Upper and Lower Teeth of
Protocyon troglodytes from Bolivia and Ecuador

Dimension		MNHN, GMT 1	UF 26911[*]	UF 26911[+]	UF 27889	MNHN, NUA 91
C	L	---	11.4	11.1e	---	---
	W	---	8.3	10.7	---	---
P_1	L	---	---	6.1e	---	---
	W	---	---	5.7e	---	---
P_2	L	10.8e	---	7.9e	---	---
	W	5.5	---	4.9	---	---
P_3	L	13.1e	---	11.6	---	---
	W	5.5	---	6.0e	---	---
P_4	L	15.1	---	13.8	15.2	---
	W	6.4	---	6.8	6.5e	---
M_1	TrL	21.4	19.7	19.2e	20.1	19.9
	TL	6.4	5.1	6.3	6.7	6.5
	TrW	11.2	9.9	8.2	10.6	10.0
M_2	TrL	---	5.7	6.3	---	5.3e
	TL	---	3.5	3.7	---	2.7e
	TrW	8.5	8.4	8.2	7.1	6.9
M_3	L	---	4.4	5.5	---	---
	W	---	4.3	5.0	---	---

[+] Right.
[*] Left.

this dimension, measuring between 30.0 and 30.3 mm. The angular process exhibits an expanded fossa for the inferior branch of the medial pterygoideus muscle.

The premolars are broken at crown level in both Tarijan specimens, and their tips are broken in MNHN GMT-1. However, the posterior half in P_{3-4} is present and suggests that these teeth were slender, relatively high-crowned, and set off by short diastemata. M_1 has a slender trigonid and lacks a metaconid. The short, narrow talonid displays a large hypoconid in a central position and a basal cingulum in the position of the entoconid. M_2 trigonid is transversely broad, with slight development of an anterolabial cingulum in the Tarijan specimens. All specimens show development of a strong paracristid. The protoconid is larger than the metaconid, with the former cusp positioned slightly behind the metaconid. M_3 is small with a circular occlusal outline.

Remarks. Canis troglodytes was established by Lund (1840a:14) on the basis of hindfoot elements (metatarsal III, phalanx I, II, III) which he illustrated on pl. 18, fig. 7. Formal description of this species was not provided by its author until 1843, when he transferred the species to his newly established genus Palaeocyon (Lund, 1843:50-54).

The following characters were used by Lund to diagnose Palaeocyon: short face, small postorbital processes, wide palate, short coronoid process, metaconid on M_1 rudimentary and entoconid absent, P_4 protocone very reduced, and short metapodials. He recognized two species, P. validus and P. troglodytes. P. validus, differentiated on the basis of its smaller size, is now recognized as a junior synonym of P. troglodytes.

In his description of P. troglodytes, Lund (1840a) figured (pls. 69 and 45) UZM L:228, left P^4; 187, right maxillary fragment with P^4-M^1; 236, right mandible with C, P_{1-3}, M_1; 251, left M^2; 249, right I_3; 248, left I_3; and 257, I_2. Since these figured specimens were the basis for his formal description, they have been designated as co-types.

Winge (1895) synonymized <u>Palaeocyon</u> under <u>Canis</u>. He figured (pls. 1 and 2) UZM L:5697–5698, right maxillary with I^3, C, P^{1-4}, M^1; 5700, right ramus with M_{1-3}; 236 (listed above); 57, astragalus; 56, calcaneum; 5756, right ulna; 6579, right ramus with C, dP_1, dP_4, P_4; 6582, right maxillary fragment with dP^{3-4}; 8088, distal right tibia; and 117, metatarsal III. His description of this species was similar to Lund's, though he noted the resemblance of P^4 and M_1 to those of <u>Cuon</u> <u>alpinus</u>.

Giebel (1855:851) transferred the genus <u>Palaeocyon</u> (Lund, 1843) to his newly established genus <u>Protocyon</u>, since the generic name <u>Palaeocyon</u> was preoccupied. Simpson (1945) and J. L. Kraglievich (1952) followed Giebel's nomenclature.

<u>Protocyon troglodytes</u> is among the best represented of the South American large canids. Although only teeth and cranial elements are described herein, Winge (1895) lists measurements for postcrania referred to this species, and L. Kraglievich lists comparative measurements for postcrania ascribed to <u>C</u>. <u>lupus</u>, <u>C</u>. <u>nehringi</u>, and <u>Canis</u> sp.

<u>Protocyon</u> cf. <u>P</u>. <u>troglodytes</u>

<u>Material</u>. MNHN TAR-658, incomplete right ramus with P_2, M_2 (C broken below crown, P_{1-4} broken at crown, M_3 alveolus).

<u>Stratigraphic and geographic distribution</u>. This referred specimen was collected by R. Hoffstetter from Tarija, Bolivia.

<u>Age</u>. Late Ensenadan and/or early Lujanian.

<u>Description</u>. The ramus is transversely narrow and deep, particularly below M_{1-2}. A large mental foramen is below the anterior root of P_2, and a smaller foramen is below the posterior root of P_3. The ascending ramus is missing. Both the canine and P_1 are broken at the crown. Judging from the P_1 alveolus, the tooth is small and offers no peculiarities. P_2 is double-rooted, elongate,

and single-cusped, terminating in a blunt heel. Similar to P_2, P_3 is longer and slightly broader posteriorly. P_4 is broken at the crown, its alveolus indicating that the tooth was double-rooted, elongate, and considerably broader posteriorly than P_3.

M_1 is relatively large and lacks a metaconid. The trigonid is twice as long as wide. The talonid is short and broad with a large hypoconid. Lingual to the hypoconid is a cingular ridge. Relative to M_1, M_2 is large. A large, conical protoconid is the only cusp present on the trigonid on M_2. The paracristid is well developed. The talonid is short and broad, with the crista obliqua connecting the protoconid to a small hypoconid. M_3 is missing, although its alveolus suggests that the tooth was relativly large, single-rooted, and ovoid in outline.

Remarks. This specimen compares most closely with P. troglodytes, but due to the absence of a metaconid on the trigonid of M_2, MNHN TAR-658 has been tentatively referred to P. cf. P. troglodytes.

Measurements. P_2, length 11.9 mm, width 5.9 mm; P_3, length 12.5 mm, width 6.2 mm; M_1, trigonid 21.4 mm long and 11.5 mm wide, talonid 6.7 mm long and 11.2 mm wide; M_2, trigonid 6.4 mm long, talonid 4.1 mm long.

Protocyon sp.

Material. MMP 417, right ramal fragment with P_4 and the anterior portion of M_1.

Stratigraphic and geographic distribution. Vorohue Formation, collected from top of drainage sewer at Camet Parque in Mar del Plata, Buenos Aires Province, Argentina.

Age. Uquian.

Description. P_4 is 12.8 mm long and 6.8 mm wide, with high, sharp cusps. A small, basal anterior cusplet and a single posterior cusplet flank the principal cusp. A small posterolingual cingulum is between the posterior cusplet and the broad, blunt heel of the tooth. M_1 is directly behind P_4, although only the anteriormost portion of the paraconid is preserved.

Remarks. MMP 417 was collected by Galileo Scaglia in 1948. The specimen is very fragmentary and is referred to Protocyon based on the presence of an anterior cusplet on P_4. P_4 dimensions are smaller than those of P. orcesi and P. troglodytes.

Chrysocyon Hamilton Smith, 1839:242

Canis Illiger, 1815:109 (partim, non Linnaeus, 1758)
Chrysocyon Hamilton Smith, 1839:242.

Type species. C. brachyurus (Illiger, 1815:109).

Geographic distribution. Fossil specimens recorded from Bolivia and Brazil

Age. Ensenadan (medial Pleistocene). Lujanian (late Pleistocene), and Holocene.

Included species. Chrysocyon brachyurus and an undescribed species (Tedford and Taylor, pers. commun.)

Revised Diagnosis. Frontal sinus large, penetrating postorbital process and extending posteriorly to the frontal-parietal suture (fig. 10); coronoid process anteroposteriorly high and dorsoventrally narrow; angular process of mandible expanded with large fossa for superior branch of medial pterygoideus muscle (Fig. 11); P^4/M_1 small relative to M^{1-2}/M_{2-3}; M^{1-2} very broad relative to their lengths; caecum straight or nearly so; limbs greatly elongated.

Chrysocyon brachyurus Illiger, 1815:109)

(Fig. 25)

Chrysocyon jubatus Desmarest, 1820:198.

Chrysocyon campestris Wied, 1826:334 (non Bechstein, 1797:__).

Chrysocyon isodacylus F. Ameghino, 1905:9.

Chrysocyon brachyurus L. Kraglievich, 1930:47; Hoffstetter, 1963a:198.

Material. Fossil material referable to this species includes: MNHN ?, humerus; and in UZM L:3039, left partial maxillary with P^{3-4}, M^1 (M_2 alveolus); 2734, parietal fragment and interparietal region; 3771, postorbital fragment; 3014, left distal two-thirds of femur; 3037, right femur (missing proximal end); 3038, left distal femur; 12501, distal tibia; 3797, left proximal tibia; 3773, right proximal ulna; 3802, radius; 3040, metapodial (proximal end missing); 3801, axis; 3775, atlas; 3788, ilium fragment; 3792, ishium fragment; 3787, 3778, 3779, 3774, 3800, lumbar vertebrae.

Stratigraphic and geographic distribution. The MNHN specimen was collected from Tarija, Bolivia, by R. H. Hoffstetter. The UZM L material was collected by P. W. Lund from a Lagoa Santa Cave, Lapa da Lagoa do Sumidouro, Minas Gerais, Brazil.

Age. Late Ensenadan or early Lujanian; Lujanian and Holocene.

Diagnosis. Same as for genus.

Description. Cranial and dental material referable to this species from the Lagoa Santa Caves were used in this description (see Table 14). Skull fragments indicate that temporal ridges are fused into a prominent interparietal crest and that the frontal sinus was large and extended behind the postorbital processes.

A maxillary fragment, UZM L3039, preserves the premolars which are simple, narrow, and set off by diastemata (Fig. 25). P^3

TABLE 14

Measurements of Cheek Teeth of Fossil
and Recent Chrysocyon brachyurus

	C. brachyurus UZM L3039		C. brachyurus Recent	
		N	$\bar{X}$	O.R.
P^3 L	11.7	3	11.6	11.3-11.8
W	6.2	3	5.2	5.0- 5.3
P^4 L	17.9	3	18.0	17.9-18.2
W	11.1	3	10.1	9.5-10.9
M^1 L	15.1	3	15.6	15.1-15.9
W	18.7	3	18.8	18.6-19.0

is double-rooted with a single large central cusp. A slight posterior swelling indicates the presence of a weak posterior cusplet. As in all recent specimens examined, P_3 broadens posteriorly. The carnassial is conspicuously small relative to M^{1-2} with a large, bulbous protocone anterolingually directed (Fig. 25). A basal lingual cingulum is well developed. M^1 is broad, especially across the talon basin. The labial cingulum is prominent only around the anterolabial portion of the paracone. Paraconule and metaconule are well developed. The protocone is anterolingually inflated to a lesser degree than in recent specimens. The large, well worn hypocone is posterlingually directed relative to the protocone. Only the M^2 alveolus is preserved, which suggests that this tooth was also broad in both anterposterior and transverse dimensions

Remarks. Langguth (1969:5) details the nomenclatural history of Chrysocyon brachyurus, of which only a summary will be presented

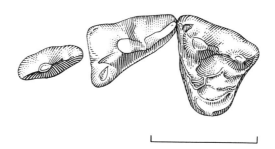

FIGURE 25. Chrysocyon brachyurus (Illiger, 1815). UZM L3039 (UCMP 123393), left partial maxillary with P^{3-4}, M^1: occlusal view. Scale = 20 mm.

here. Illiger (1815:109) was the first to describe the Maned Wolf as a new species of Canis, Canis brachyurus. Desmarest (1820:198) described the same material and employed the name Canis jubatus. Osgood (1919) pointed out that the name Canis brachyurus had priority by date of publication over Canis jubatus. F. Ameghino (1905) proposed the subgenus Chrysocyon on the basis of certain cranial and dental characters he observed in a skeleton at MACN and referred this specimen to Canis (Chrysocyon) isodactylus. This species was later reassigned by L. Kraglievich (1930:46) as a junior synonym of Chrysocyon brachyurus.

Winge (1895:24) recorded the presence of this genus in the Lagoa Santa Caves and found the material indistinguishable from the living species. Since these cave deposits range in age from Lujanian to Holocene, it is not possible to document with certainty that this represents a fossil occurrence. Hoffstetter (1963a:198), however, records a humerus which he refers to C. brachyurus from Tarija, Bolivia.

Caninae sp. indet.

Material. MLP 52-IX-27-10, left ramal fragment with C, P_{1-2}.

Stratigraphic and geographic distribution.   "Pampean Formation," collected from Rio Salado, near Esperanza, Santa Fe Province, Argentina.

Age. Lujanian.

Description.   The canine is small and robust, though only the basal half of the crown is represented.   An anterolingual wear surface is developed.   The wear pattern suggests that the tooth was broken during the life of the individual, exposing the pulp cavity. P_1 is small, single-rooted, and single-cusped, and an extensive wear surface is produced posterolingually. P_2 is double-rooted and single-cusped; the tip of the crown is worn, as well as the heel.

Measurements.   C, 10.5 mm long, 6.8 mm wide; P_1, 6.5 mm long, 5.2 mm wide; P_2, 11.0 mm long, 5.5 mm wide.

Remarks.   MLP 52-IX-27-10 was collected by Joaquin Frenguelli in 1929.   As evident from the diagnoses of Canis, Theriodictis, Protocyon and Chrysocyon, the posterior premolars and molars are more useful for identification purposes than are the canine and the anterior premolars. The tooth measurements of MLP 52-IX-27-10 fall into a size range comparable with Theriodictis platensis; however, the sample size of South American larger canids is too small to allow for further taxonomic refinement, other than assignment of this specimen to the subfamily Caninae.

PHYLOGENETIC RELATIONSHIPS

Phylogenetic relationships among South American canids and related taxa are represented in a cladogram (Fig. 26). Shared derived characters upon which these relationships are based are

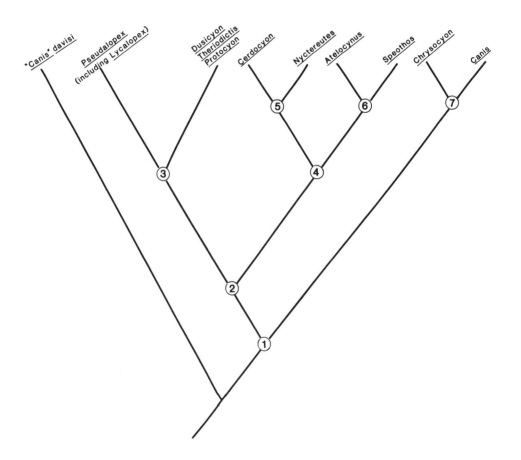

Figure 26. Cladogram of proposed relationships among South American canids and related taxa.

listed below together with numerical reference to more complete character descriptions (see section on Character Analysis, above).

South American canids are most closely related to the North American canid "Canis" davisi. Derived characters which distinguish this group of advanced canids from "Canis" davisi are the following (Fig. 26, point 1): (a) strongly arched zygomata with inverted jugals (3) and (b) angular process large, with expanded fossa for inferior/superior branch of medial pterygoideus muscle or expanded pterygoid fossa (10).

Three groups of South American canids are recognized: Dusicyon, Cerdocyon, and Canis clades. The Dusicyon and Cerdocyon clades are united by possession of the following characters (Fig. 26, point 2): (a) long palatines extending to or beyond toothrow (5), (b) coronoid process anteroposteriorly broad and dorsoventrally low (11), (c) Ml with protostylid (28), (d) Ml_{-2} with mesoconid (29), and (e) M_2 with strong paracristid (32).

Members of the Dusicyon clade — which includes the foxes Dusicyon and Pseudalopex (including Lycalopex) and their sister taxa, the large fossil canids Protocyon and Theriodictis — share the following character (fig. 26, point 2; fig. 27, point 1): frontal sinus large, does not penetrate postorbital process (1), differs in Theriodictis.

Fig. 27 presents in more detail relationships among members of the Dusicyon clade. Preliminary study of living and fossil South American foxes indicates that the large culpeo foxes, the Falkland Island Wolf Dusicyon australis (Kerr, 1792), and Dusicyon avus (Burmeister, 1864) are closely related to Theriodictis and Protocyon. Dusicyon, Theriodictis, and Protocyon share the following derived characters (fig. 27, point 2): (a) broad palate (6), (b) deep zygomata with wide masseteric scar (2), (c) P^4 with reduced, low protocone in posterolingual orientation, with rounded anterolabial border (16), (d) small $M^2/_2$ relative to $M^1/_1$ (31), (e) P_3 crown with posterior tilt (25). (f) M_1 metaconid reduced (27), and (g) M_2 metaconid relatively unreduced (33).

Theriodictis and Protocyon share the following characters (fig. 27, point 3): (a) M^1 with reduced hypocone (22b), (b) M^2 with reduced metacone (23), and (c) M_1 metaconid absent (27b).

Protocyon is distinguished by (fig. 27, point 5): (a) M^{1-2} hypocone absent (22b), and (b) M_1 metaconid and entoconid absent $(27b_2)$.

Protocyon scagliarum is the earliest recorded wolf-like canid from South America. The occurrence of this derived species, together with the first appearance of a derived member of the South American fox complex, Cerdocyon, in the late Hemphillian of North America (Tedford and Taylor, pers. commun., 1978; Torres and Ferrusquia, 1981), and its sister taxon, Nyctereutes, in coeval deposits of late Miocene age in Europe, suggests the probable differentiation of this lineage in North and Middle America prior to establishment of the Panamanian land bridge and their entry into South America. This Uquian species, P. scagliarum, is distinguished from other members of this lineage in having anterior lower premolars set off by a diastemata, and P_4 with anterior and posterior cusplets. P. troglodytes and P. orcesi, recorded from Ensenadan and Lujanian age deposits, respectively, are united in having overlapping anterior lower premolars; P. orcesi can be distinguished by loss of M_3, interpreted as the derived condition.

As suggested, the Protocyon group is most closely related to the South American foxes Dusicyon and Pseudalopex. Members of this group are known as far back as the Ensenadan, and presumably formed the "ancestral" stock from which both Protocyon and its sister taxon Theriodictis were derived. It should be noted that although no close phylogenetic relationship is suggested between the Theriodictis-Protocyon lineage and the reported North American Cuon species (Nowak and Kortlucke, pers. commun. 1984), these genera share several convergent characters, among the most important of which is simplification of the M_1 talonid with reduction and/or loss of metaconid and entoconid.

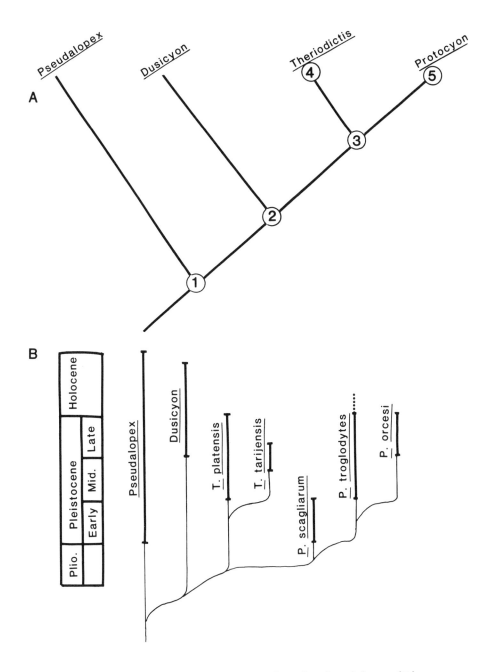

Figure 27. (A) Cladogram of proposed relationships (B) stratigraphic and presumed phylogenetic relationships among Pseudalopex, Dusicyon, Theriodictis, and Protocyon. Vertical lines indicate stratigraphic range of each taxon; dashed lines express relationships.

Theriodictis platensis makes a good morphologic ancestor for
Protocyon.   It retains several primitive dental characters,
modified among *Protocyon* species, including loss of the metaconid
on M_1, simplification of the M_1 talonid with the entoconid
retained as a distinct cusp, M^{1-2} with reduced hypocones, and M_3
present.

The *Cerdocyon* clade, which includes the South American foxes
and dogs *Cerdocyon*, *Atelocynus*, and *Speothos* and the Asian raccoon
dog *Nyctereutes*, is united by possession of the following
characters (fig. 26, point 4): (a) external auditory meatus very
short and of small diameter (8), (b) angular process with
pterygoid fossa greatly expanded (Type D of Gaspard, 1964, fig.
24) (10), (c) subangular lobe present (9), (d) M^{1-2} very narrow
for their length (17), (e) ears short (35), (f) caecum short and
straight (36), and (g) legs very short (37).

The *Cerdocyon* clade is currently under investigation (Tedford
and Taylor, pers. commun., 1978; Berta, in prep.).   Among
characters discussed in this study *Cerdocyon* and *Nyctereutes* are
linked as sister taxa by joint possession of (fig. 26, point 4):
P^4/M_1 small relative to M^{1-2}/M_{2-3} (15).   *Cerdocyon* is distinguished, among other characters, by having palatines that are much
shorter than the toothrow.   *Atelocynus* and *Speothos* share a
derived character (fig. 27, point 5): frontal sinus small, does
not penetrate postorbital process (1).   *Speothos* is distinguished
by the loss of $M^2/_3$.

The *Canis* clade, as discussed here includes the South American "wolf" *Chrysocyon* and its sister taxon *Canis*. These taxa share
the following derived characters (Fig. 26, point 6): (a) frontal
sinus large, penetrating postorbital process, extending anteriorly
and particularly posteriorly ultimately to the frontal-parietal
suture (1), (b) angular process with large fossa for superior
branch of medial pterygoideus muscle (10), and (c) I^3 enlarged,
with accessory cusps and strong posteromedial cingulum (12).

The *Chrysocyon* lineage includes a fossil species from
the Blancan of Arizona and Mexico (Tedford, pers. commun.) and the

extant species $\underline{C}$. brachyurus, known from Lujanian-Holocene age deposits in Bolivia and Brazil. Chrysocyon is distinguished from Canis in having: (a) P^4/M_1 small relative to M^{1-2}/M_{2-3} (15), (b) caecum short and straight (36), and (c) Limbs greatly elongate (37).

Hypothesized species-level relationships among the Canis lineage are represented in Fig. 28. South American fossil representatives of the Canis group include $\underline{C}$. gezi, $\underline{C}$. nehringi, and $\underline{C}$. dirus, and they show closest affinity with North American Pleistocene species. The shared derived character which unites $\underline{C}$. armbrusteri and the Eurasian wolf $\underline{C}$. falconeri is (Fig. 28, point 2): P_4 with an additional posterior cusplet on the cingular shelf (26), $\underline{C}$. falconeri is distinguished by: M^{1-2} labial cingulum reduced (19). $\underline{C}$. gezi shares with later canids the following character (Fig. 28, point 3): Wide palate (6). $\underline{C}$. gezi and North American $\underline{C}$. cf. $\underline{C}$. dirus are united as sister taxa by (Fig. 28, point 4) more anterior position of the hypocone relative to the protocone on M^1 (21). $\underline{C}$. cf. $\underline{C}$. dirus is more derived, relative to $\underline{C}$. gezi, by: $P^3/_3$ with two posterior cusplets (14). $\underline{C}$. nehringi and $\underline{C}$. dirus share the following derived characters (Fig. 28, point 5): (a) narrow, triangular supraoccipital shield with an overhanging inion (4), (b) anterolingual cingulum seldom extending around the protocone of M^1 (24), and (c) anterior lacerate foramen and optic foramen in common pit (7).

$\underline{C}$. dirus is derived, relative to $\underline{C}$. nehringi, by (Fig. 28, point 6): (a) $P^2/_2$ with a posterior cusplet (14), (b) P^3 with two posterior cusplets (14), (c) M_1 with metastylid, entocristid, entoconulid, and transverse crest extending from metaconid to hypoconid (27), and (d) M_2 with entocristid and entoconulid (27).

The earliest well documented Canis, $\underline{C}$. gezi, appears in the Ensenadan and serves as a very advanced morphologic ancestor for later species. This late record suggests either a prior, as yet unrecorded history of the group on the continent, or presence of a very advanced ancestral morphotype, having an earlier history elsewhere. From what little is known of the evolutionary history

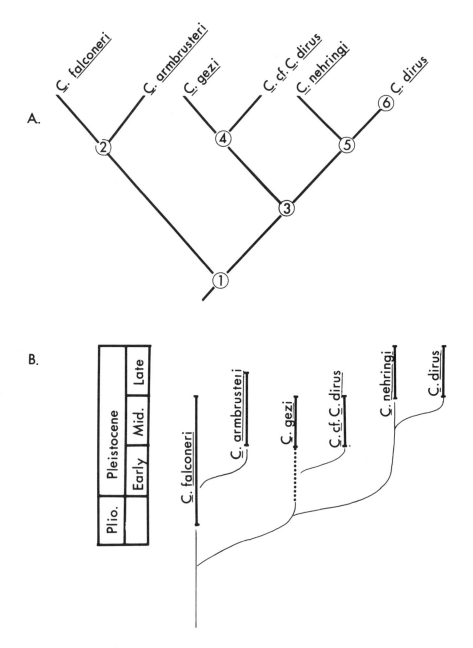

Figure 28. (A) Cladogram of proposed relationships (B) stratigraphic and presumed phylogenetic relationships among North American, Eurasian, and South American Pleistocene Canis. Vertical lines indicate stratigraphic range of each taxon; dotted lines indicate questionable stratigraphic range; dashed lines express relationships.

America, the latter suggestion is more likely. It is probable that sometime after appearance of the Panamerican land bridge, three million years ago, an ancestral form similar to C. gezi arrived as an immigrant from North America. Such an ancestor would have been moderate to large in size with broad skull proportions, elongate premolars, and large carnassials with a bicuspid talonid on M_1.

C. gezi is most closely related to Irvingtonian C. cf. C. dirus (sensu Tedford and Taylor, pers. commun., 1978), and is a good structural ancestor for the Lujanian species C. nehringi. The primary changes acquired by C. nehringi include continuation of the trend toward large size, development of a narrow, triangular supraoccipital shield, and greater complication of cusps on the upper and lower molars. This latter character is interpreted as a trend toward hypocarnivory.

C. nehringi coexisted with C. dirus, the latter species appearing during the same time interval, late Pleistocene, in both North and South America. C. dirus is more derived than C. nehringi in its larger size, more massive proportions, and more complex construction of the lower molars with numerous additional cusps on the talonid. Presumably, these characters were adaptations to an increasingly efficient predaceous habit.

Tedford and Taylor (pers. commun., 1978) suggest that in North America, the Irvingtonian wolf C. cf. C. dirus may represent the stock from which the Rancholabrean C. dirus evolved. Earlier, Kurten (1967) suggested that C. falconeri, a large wolf from the late Pliocene of Eurasia, might be closely related to C. dirus, and Martin (1974) proposed that C. armbrusteri (recognized by him as synonymous with C. lupus) may have evolved into this species. Characters evaluated on the preceding pages and the accompanying cladogram indicate that C. dirus is most closely related to C. nehringi and it shares a more distant relationship with C. cf. C. dirus, C. armbrusteri, and C. falconeri.

BIOGEOGRAPHY

The evolutionary history of the Canidae, indeed the entire Order Carnivora, in South America is intimately tied to emergence of the Panamanian land bridge linking this continent with North America. The timing of this connection is widely disputed. Unfortunately, the known tectonic history of the isthmus is of little help in offering a timetable of events. Webb (1978) admirably reviews diverse geologic and biologic evidence concerning closure of the isthmus and the beginning of faunal interchange. The various proposed dates, based on the age and geographic affinities of marine fossil assemblages on both sides of the isthmus, range from the late Miocene to the middle Pliocene (e.g., Whitmore and Stewart, 1965; Woodring, 1966). Recent planktonic foraminiferal biogeography and paleoceanography (including carbon-isotopic data) provide a range of suggested minimum dates for closure of the isthmus during the middle Pliocene from 4.0-3.0 mybp (Keigwin, 1978, 1982).

With regard to data offered by land vertebrates, there are two schools of thought. The "old school" championed by Hershkovitz (1966, 1969, 1972), and more recently by Savage (1974), advocates faunal interchange prior to a land-bridge connection 10-12 mybp (late Miocene). The principal line of evidence in support of this view contrasts the exceptional diversification shown by present-day cricetid rodents (more than 40 genera are currently recognized-Hershkovitz, 1972) with their presumed late date of arrival (Montehermosan, early Pliocene) on the South American continent. Proponents of this view claim that more time was needed for such extensive taxonomic diversity and evolutionary change than the fossil record documents (Hershkovitz, 1962, 1972; Savage, 1974). Additionally, these workers argue that the earliest fossil forms are too advanced to be considered the first immigrants, suggesting an earlier radiation in northern South America where there is no fossil record.

Marshall (1979b), expanding on an earlier suggestion of Simpson (1950) and Patterson and Pascual (1972), proposes that cricetid rodents evolved in North America and immigrated into South America, arriving by waif dispersal across the Bolivar trough 7.0-5.0 mybp.   Once in South America, according to Marshall, they underwent a major adaptive radiation in the savanna grassland areas of Venezuela, Columbia, and the Guianas, where they remained restricted until about 3.5 mybp.   At that time, the first major glaciation in South America resulted in the expansion of savanna grassland habitats.   Presumably, cricetids then spread through a savanna grassland corridor into Bolivia and Argentina. As yet this model is not supported by the fossil record, which indicates that the first cricetids entered the continent in Chapadmalalan and Montehermosan times.   In addition, recognition of certain fossil cricetids in the southwestern United States suggests diversification in North and Middle America prior to their South American immigration (Baskin, 1978; Jacobs, 1977; Jacobs and Lindsay, 1981).

The "young school" founded by Simpson (1950), elaborated by Patterson and Pascual (1972), and followed today by most vertebrate paleontologists, advocates a land connection beginning about 3 mybp.   More than 30 vertebrate genera are involved in the interchange between North and South America.   Correlation of North and South American late Cenozoic land-mammal ages is dependent upon the reliability of biostratigraphic comparisons of taxa that made the interchange, since relatively few radioisotopic dates are available for this portion of the time scale (see Fig. 1).

Beginning of the interchange in South America is marked by appearance of a single procyonid genus, Cyonasua, in Huayquerian (middle Miocene) age deposits of Argentina.   A series of potassium-argon dates were obtained by Marshall et al. (1979) on volcanic-ash deposits which bracket Cyonasua occurrences in Argentina between 7.5-9.5 mybp.   In North America, the immigrants include three ground-sloth genera representing two different families: Megalonyx and Pliometanastes (megalonychids), and

Thinobadistes (a mylodontid). The earliest reliably dated sloth in California is from the early Hemphillian Mehrten Formation (8.19 ± 0.16 mybp) (Hirschfeld, 1981).

As Webb (1978:407) observes, each of these mammal groups is noted for its broad ecologic tolerances and dispersal ability over water, suggesting that they may have crossed water barriers about 6 million years before the land bridge was completed. Early crossings by Cyonasua and the three ground-sloth genera mentioned above are often marshalled as evidence supporting early completion of the Panamanian land bridge.

Earliest evidence for renewed faunal interchange between the Americas comes from the Chapadmalalan (late Pliocene). The Chapadmalalan and Montehermosan record the presence in South America of the procyonid Chapalmalania, presumably derived from a Cyonasua-like ancestor; a hognosed skunk, Conepatus; a sigmodontine mouse, Proreithrodon; and a peccary, Agyrohyus. In late Blancan faunas of North America dated about 2.5 mybp, the southern mammalian emigrants include a member of the porcupine family, Coendou; the armadillos Kraglievichia and Dasypus; a large ground sloth, Glossotherium; a capybara, Neochoerus; and a manatee, Trichechus. The phororhacid ground bird Titanis is also present.

The next wave of faunal interchange was during the Uquian, the acme of northern dispersals into South America, which correlates in part with latest Blancan and early to middle Irvingtonian in North America. Between 11 and 14 genera are recorded in South America, representing the following northern families: Canidae, Ursidae, Felidae, Equidae, Camelidae, Gomphotheriidae, Tapiridae, and Cervidae. Irvingtonian faunas of North America include the following immigrants from the south: an oppossum, Didelphis; a giant armadillo, Pampatherium; a capybara, Hydrochoerus; and two ground sloths, Eremotherium and Nothrotheriops.

The next land-mammal age in South America, the Ensenadan, records three genera: the otter, Lutra; two large cats, Felis onca and F. concolor; and Equus. Webb (1976:223) has noted that, with the exception of Equus, these genera lack probable ancestors in

South America and have nearly contemporaneous records in North America, suggesting that they first arrived in South America at this time.   The late Ensenadan and Lujanian land mammal age in South America are correlated with late Irvingtonian and Rancholabrean North American faunas, and neither records any new northern immigrants into South America.

The Canis and Theriodictis-Protocyon lineages have been studied in sufficient detail to trace their probable centers of evolution and dispersal.   The biogeographic hypotheses discussed below are based upon phylogenetic interpretations previously formulated.   Both vicariance and dispersal models are evoked.

The evolutionary history of Canis suggests that the ancestral species group (including C. etruscus, C. cipio, and C. michaux; see Torre, 1979) was distributed over Holarctica between 7-4 mypb. A vicariant event-repeated openings of the Bering Land Bridge, which occurred between 3.5-1.5 mybp-isolated derived members of this group, C. falconeri in Eurasia and C. armbrusteri in North America.   During the time interval extending from 1.0-10,000 mybp, derived representatives of the genus Canis dispersed from North America to South Amerca via the Panamanian land bridge. From this derived wolf stock (including C. armbrusteri and C. cf. C. dirus) evolved C. gezi and later C. nehringi and C. dirus.

There is no conclusive evidence that can be offered in determining whether the dire wolf originated in North or South America.   A North American center of origin is favored for several reasons.   While the fossil record documents the presence of primitive wolf stock in South America during the middle Pleistocene (e.g., C. gezi), members of this basal group are much better represented in North America (e.g., C. cf. C. dirus, C. armbrusteri).   As previously mentioned, known South American occurrences of C. dirus are limited to localities in Talara, Peru; Muaco, Venezuela; and Quebrada del Puente Alto, Bolivia.   In comparison, North America's record of this species shows it more widely distributed throughout the continent, from Alaska to Mexico and from California to Florida (Fig. 29).

Figure 29. Records of occurrence of <u>Canis</u> <u>dirus</u>. Shaded area represents the eastern savanna dispersal route; unshaded area represents the Andean dispersal route. (For complete descriptions of North American localities see Nowak, 1979 and for South America see text). Localities 1-7 are in Mexico and late Pleistocene in age: 1, San Josecito Cave, near Aramberri, Nuevo Leon; 2, Lago de Chapala, Jalisco; 3, Near Tequixquiac, Mexico; 4, Valsequillo, near Puebla, Mexico; 5, Cedazo, Aguascalientes, Mexico; 6, El Tajo Quarry, Mexico; 7, Comondu, Baja California del Sur. Localities 8-10 are in South America and late Pleistocene in age: 8, Muaco, Falcon State, Venezuela; 9, Talara, Piura Dept., Peru; 10, Quebrada del Puente Alto, near Tarija, Tarija Dept., Bolivia.

The distribution of C. dirus suggests that it followed the Andean corridor or "high road" which served as a direct north-south dispersal route in South America. According to Webb (1978:413), this Andean route extended along the Andean chain from the isthmian region and provided a pathway for temperate bird and mammal groups to pass from Central America into South America. It is characterized by cool, dry, unforested habitats. Pacific coastal lowland faunas such as Talara, Peru, and La Carolina, Ecuador, are included along the pathway of the Andean route. These regions have experienced alternating wet and dry climate during the late Cenozoic, and their rich and diverse fossil assemblages are in marked contrast with the relatively depauperate present-day faunas. Though traffic along the Andean route continues to flourish, the dire wolf became extinct on both continents at the end of the Pleistocene, and the Canis lineage survives only in North America.

The Theriodictis-Protocyon lineage offers a different biogeographic history, and one need only evoke the dispersal model to explain its distribution. Representatives of this lineage are most closely related to the South American foxes Dusicyon and Pseudalopex and suggest evolution of this group in North and Middle America, with maximum diversification on the southern continent. Although these foxes are unknown from the North American fossil record, a more derived member of this group, Cerdocyon, is recorded from the late Hemphillian and early Blancan (6-3 mybp-late Miocene-early Pliocene) of Texas and Mexico (Tedford and Taylor, pers. commun., 1978; Torres and Ferrusquia, 1981). The appearance of the very derived taxon Protocyon in early Pleistocene deposits further suggests a prior, as yet unrecorded history of this group in Middle America. It seems likely that much of the differentiation of these foxes may have taken place in Middle America, where sampling is poor.

The Theriodictis-Protocyon lineage dispersed across the Panamanian land bridge from North and/or Middle America into South America and then differentiated and radiated into Bolivia, Brazil,

Ecuador, and Argentina. The Falkland Island Wolf Dusicyon australis represents a specialized offshoot of this radiation which survived into the Recent.

The Theriodictis-Protocyon lineage probably dispersed along both the Andean route and the eastern savanna route in South America. The majority of mammalian taxa presumably took the former route, with several traversing the eastern savanna route, which extends from the Caribbean perimeter of Central America into eastern Venezuela and then crosses the Amazon basin and passes southward into Argentina, where it joins the Andean route. Savanna habitats predominate along this route. Several faunas which record members of the Protocyon lineage also include amphibious and browsing mammals such as Haplomastodon, Eremotherium, and Stegomastodon (Muaco, Venezuela, and Lagoa Santa Caves, Brazil) which probably followed this route.

Chrysocyon appears to have originated in North America during the late Miocene/early Pliocene (Tedford, pers. commun., 1982). The earliest reported occurrence of this genus in South America is from the middle Pleistocene of Bolivia. The more extensive present-day range of the Maned Wolf indicates subsequent dispersal of this animal into Paraguay, Uruguay and northern Argentina.

CARNIVORE ADAPTIVE ZONES

An attempt was made to define and compare late Cenozoic and present-day occupation of carnivore adaptive zones in South America (Fig. 30). Usage of the term "adaptive zone" follows Van Valen (1971:421), and the principal criteria used to define it were body size, feeding specialization, and hunting strategy.

Marshall (1979a) documents early to late Tertiary occupation of carnivore adaptive zones in South America by the dog-like marsupial family Borhyaenidae. As he suggests, the stratigraphic record indicates that this group was apparently extinct before the first placental carnivores appear in the record. This supports the view that the Borhyaenidae were ecologically replaced by placental carnivores which came to occupy a similar role during the Pleistocene.

Among the South American Pleistocene large canids, there were apparently three adaptive trends. The _Canis_ group had relatively

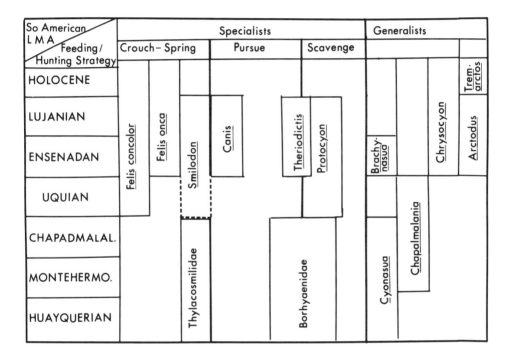

Figure 30. Generalized diagram showing occupation of the carnivore adaptive zone in South America during the late Cenozoic and in the present for large to intermediate sized carnivores and large to intermediate sized omnivores. Stratigraphic ranges are those compiled by Berta and Marshall, 1978.

long, broad skulls and rostra, elongate premolars, large carnassials, and bicuspid talonids, emphasizing both shearing and
crushing masticatory functions. The Theriodictis-Protocyon group,
with its shortened skulls and rostra, high crowned premolars, and
trenchant M_1 with very reduced or absent metaconids and ento-
conids, exemplified a trend toward simplification of the talonid
and increasing specialization of the shearing mechanism. These
genera illustrate trends suggestive of highly predaceous habits.
Chrysocyon, with its long, shallow skull and rostrum, weak
canines, short carnassials, broad M^{1-2}, and bicuspid talonids,
illustrates an omnivorous habit.

These canid groups can be divided into two adaptive zones
based on size and feeding specialization: a large to intermediate
sized carnivore zone, comprising the Canis an Theriodictis-
Protocyon groups and a large to intermediate sized omnivore zone,
the Chrysocyon group. These adaptive zones will be discussed in
considerable detail, whereas only brief mention will be given the
other adaptive zone recognized, that of the small omnivore-
carnivore. Members of the Canidae as well as representatives of
other carnivore families occupied these zones. I have followed
Keast (1977) in further subdividing occupants of the large-to-
intermediate-sized carnivore zone, so-called "specialists," into:
(a) crouch-and-spring hunters, (b) pursuit hunters, and (c)
scavengers (that usually do a little hunting). "Generalists" are
here considered occupants of the omnivore zone (Fig. 30).

I. Large to Intermediate Sized Carnivore Zone

In addition to the Canis and Theriodictis-Protocyon groups,
the large to intermediate sized carnivore zone during the
Pleistocene was occupied by large cats, Felis onca, F. concolor,
and the sabercat Smilodon. The canids, true cats, and sabercat
can be separated on the basis of their feeding and hunting
strategies.

The large canids discussed here, with the exception of Chrysocyon, show dental specializations which demonstrate their ability to effectively kill prey and slice through flesh. Canids are cursorial, and their usual hunting method involves swift running.

In cats, the carnassials are further modified as highly efficient shearing blades. Loss of the metaconid and talonid on the lower carnassial, and the small size and anterior position of the protocone on P^4, are the principal modifications seen. The elongated canines of both marsupial and placental sabercats were further specialized for use in stabbing and/or slicing prey (see Simpson, 1941; Turnbull, 1978). This sabertooth specialization suggests occupation of a slightly different feeding and hunting niche from that of true cats. In contrast to canids, hunting in cats involves preliminary stalking and then a quick rush (crouch and spring), further separating the two carnivore groups from direct competition for food resources.

With regard to the fossil record of large carnivores, the last appearance of the marsupial sabercats (family Thylacosmilidae) in beds of Chapadmalalan age, and the first appearance of placental sabercats in immediately overlying beds, suggests ecologic replacement (Marshall, 1978). Several fossil species of the puma have been reported from Ensenadan and Lujanian-age deposits in Argentina and Bolivia, and four fossil subspecies of the jaguar are recorded from the Lujanian of Ecuador, Chile, and Argentina.

Today, in contrast with the past, only representatives of the crouch-and-spring guild (jaguar and puma) comprise the large to intermediate sized carnivore zone. One also notes that at the present time South America lacks any hyaenid counterpart-large-bodied scavengers and hunters with exceptionally massive jaws and teeth for crushing bone. In the Tertiary, this scavenging niche was filled in part by the Borhyaenidae and heavy-billed predacious ground birds, the phororhacids. In the Pleistocene, Theriodictis and Protocyon were partial occupants of this zone. Inquiry into the decrease in number and diversity of large carnivores in the crouch-and-spring guild, and the lack of large-bodied scavengers, must consider the simultaneous reduction in number and diversity of their specialized prey, the large herbivores.

Simpson (1962) introduced the terms "saturated," "unsaturated," and "supersaturated" to describe the ecological composition of faunas. When a fauna lacks certain basic ecologic components, it is considered unsaturated. According to Keast (1972), one of the best examples of an unsaturated fauna today is the large-herbivore fauna of Neotropica (Central and South America). Today there are only 20 species of artiodactyls and perissodactyls in Neotropica, compared to 95 in Africa. However, if we consider land area, we find that South America has only 58% of the land area of Africa. Strictly on the basis of area, then, 55 species might be expected. However, the main herbivore habitats-woodland, grassland, and arid grassland-cover about 80% of Africa, compared to 60-65% of Neotropica. This means that a total of 30-35 species is more in line with expectations. Using this reasoning, the large-herbivore fauna of South America is definitely unsaturated and markedly deficient compared to what it was throughout the Tertiary.

Keast (1972) uses the above information to support his suggestion that South America today is ecologically less sophisticated than Africa in development of its large-carnivore fauna, a consequence of the fact that it represents an earlier stage of faunal evolution.

Reduction of the large-carnivore and ungulate faunas in South America began at the end of the Pleistocene and was marked by major extinctions of large ungulates, prey for large predators such as Canis, Theriodictis, Protocyon, and Smilodon. In South America, all of the large endemic herbivores, including ground sloths, litopterns, notoungulates, and several large rodents, disappeared at this time, and in addition about half of the immigrant herbivore genera from the north, including the Equidae and Proboscidea, also became extinct. The pattern of diversity within the large to intermediate sized carnivore-adaptive zone, then, is one of diminution, especially marked at the end of the Pleistocene, as a result of large-scale extinction of the herbivore megafauna.

II. Large to Intermediate—Sized Omnivore Zone

The large to intermediate sized omnivore zone (generalists, Fig. 30) is presently occupied by the Maned Wolf Chrysocyon and the spectacled bear Tremarctos. Both of these animals are characterized as having broad, flattened, low-cusped molars adapted for crushing and grinding rather than cutting.

Chrysocyon inhabits open, grassy savannas in central and southeastern Brazil, reaching as far south as Paraguay, eastern Bolivia, and northern Argentina. Its diet consists of small mammals and birds. Tremarctos ornatus inhabits the mountainous regions of western Bolivia. It is mainly a forest animal, but often ranges into savannas of both Andean and lower elevations. Its diet is largely herbivorous, composed of leaves, roots, and fruits, but also includes deer, guanacos, and vicunas.

During the Pleistocene, Chrysocyon, Cyonasua, Brachynasua, the bear-like Chapalmalania, and Arctodus were principal occupants of this zone. Cyonasua, reported from Huayquerian-age deposits, is the earliest placental carnivore recorded from South America. Four fossil species of this genus are recorded from Argentina. Chapalmalania, first recorded from the Chapadmalalan, was convergent in size and probably feeding specialization with the borhyaenid Stylocynus (Marshall, 1978:714). A fossil species of Brachynasua is recorded from the Ensenadan of Argentina. Ten species of Arctodus are reported from Ensenadan and Lujanian-age deposits in Argentina, Bolivia, Brazil, and Uruguay. The large to intermediate sized omnivore zone was less severely affected by the major extinction event at the end of the Pleistocene, in large part due to the fact that its occupants were not dependent on herbivore megafauna for food.

III.   Small-Sized Omnivore-Carnivore Zone

Canid occupants of this zone include the bush dog Speothos, the small-eared dog Atelocynus, and the foxes Cerdocyon and Pseudalopex. The living species of bush dog, S. venaticus, is described by Langguth (1975) as a ground-dwelling carnivore predator in the forest and forest edge, inhabiting Panama, the Guianas, Colombia, Brazil, Paraguay, eastern Peru, and northern Bolivia. Its principal prey are small and large mammals and birds. Presumably the fossil species S. pacivorus, which lived from the Lujanian to the Holocene, occupied a similar ecologic role and habitat (Berta, 1984).

Cerdocyon and Pseudalopex have occupied this zone from medial Pleistocene times to the present (Berta, 1982). The single living species of the crab-eating fox, Cerdocyon thous is an inhabitant of open woodlands and grasslands in South America as far south as southern Brazil, southeastern Bolivia, Paraguay, northern Argentina, and Uruguay. Its diet consists of small rodents (field mice, rats), insects (grasshoppers), fruits (banana, mango, nuts, berries), frogs, and crabs.

Four species divided into 12 subspecies of the South American fox Pseudalopex inhabit flat, open areas and woodlands throughout the continent. Their diet is omnivorous; rodents, rabbits, birds, insects, fruits, frogs, and lizards are consumed.

The grey fox Urocyon and the small-eared dog Atelocynus are also among occupants of this zone, but unfortunately we do not have any fossil record. Atelocynus inhabits rainforests of the Amazon Basin in Peru, Brazil, Ecuador, and Colombia, and extends its range into the upper Rio Orinoco basin in Colombia and probably Venezuela. Small mammals and fruit make up its diet.

Other present-day occupants of this zone also lacking a fossil record include the procyonids Procyon, Nasua, Bassaricyon, and Potos. The living neotropical species of raccoon, Procyon cancrivorus, inhabits streamside woodlands of Costa Rica, Panama, and northern South America. It is omnivorous, but prefers aquatic life such as frogs, small land animals, and various nuts, seeds, and fruits. The coatamundi Nasua nasua is found throughout most of South America in wooded areas, feeding on available plants and small animals. A single species of kinkajou, Potos flavus, inhabits forests of southern Mexico, Central America, and south to central Brazil. Fruit is the mainstay of its diet, though insects and small mammals are also consumed. The olingo Bassaricyon gabbi is found in the jungles of Central America and northern South America. Its diet consists of fruit and small mammals.

Among mustelids occupying this zone is the grison Galictis recorded from Argentina in Uquian-Holocene deposits. This animal, weasel-like in appearance, is an inhabitant of open country or savanna. It eats a variety of food but is mainly carnivorous, preying upon small rodents.

The skunk-like Patagonian weasel Lyncodon, recorded from Ensenadan-age deposits in Argentina, is present today in this zone, as is the hognosed skunk Conepatus, first recorded from the Chapadmalalan of Argentina. Lyncodon patagonicus, living in Argentina and Chile, prefers a savanna habitat. This slender-bodied and shortlegged weasel preys upon small mammals, particularly rodents. Conepatus is the only genus of skunk in South America, but ranges from the southwestern United States to the Straits of Magellan. Wooded and open areas are inhabited, and one species is found at higher elevations on the altiplano. Its principal food is insects and grubs, though small vertebrates, including snakes and fruit, are eaten as well. Seven fossil species are recorded from Argentina, Brazil, Bolivia, and Peru.

Other present-day occupants of this zone include among the smaller cats, the ocelot Felts pardalis, marguay F. wiedi, and spotted cat F. tigrina, inhabitants of the Brazilian subregion. Ground birds and rodents, particularly caviomorphs are mainstays of their diets. Another inhabitant is the jaguarundi F. yagouroundi, which ranges from the southern United States into northern Argenina.

The small-sized omnivore-carnivore zone, in contrast to the other adaptive zones, has continued to maintain its diversity throughout the Pleistocene and into the Recent. It seems that selection has favored those carnivores having generalized omnivorous dentitions and hence more flexible feeding habits, allowing them to adapt more easily to changes, especially those at the end of the Pleistocene.

SUMMARY

The family Canidae was involved in the Plio-Pleistocene faunal interchange between North and South America. This group is well documented from deposits that range in age from Uquian (early Pleistocene) through Holocene, and was distributed in Argentina, Bolivia, Brazil, Ecuador, Peru, and Venezuela.

The large fossil canids discussed here include Canis Linnaeus, 1758; Theriodictis Mercerat, 1891; Protocyon Giebel, 1855; and Chrysocyon Hamilton Smith, 1839. These genera are distinguished from each other on the basis of cranial and mandibular characters which include: presence and degree of expansion of the frontal sinus; type of angular process; shape of the coronoid process; relative length of palatines; palatal width; and presence or absence of a subangular lobe. Diagnostic cheek-tooth characters include: length and height of premolars; large or reduced hypocone on M^{1-2}; size of protocone on P^4; bicuspid or trenchant M_1 talonid with reduction and/or loss of metaconid and entoconid; presence of a weak or strong paracristid and/or anterolabial cingulum on M_2.

Phylogenetic relationships of these genera have been summarized using cladistic analysis. Three major lineages are recognized. The Canis lineage includes three species: C. dirus Leidy, 1858; C. gezi L. Kraglievich, 1928; and C. nehringi (F. Ameghino, 1902), and they show closest relationship with North American Pleistocene Canis species.

Presumably Canis entered South America sometime during the late Pliocene or early Pleistocene. C. gezi, the most primitive species known, makes an excellent structural ancestor for the Lujanian (late Pleistocene) form C. nehringi. From this basal stock, the most advanced New World Canis species, C. dirus, can be derived. The dire wolf, known from both North and South America, probably had a North American center of origin. The entire Canis lineage became extinct at the end of the Pleistocene in South America.

A second lineage, represented by Theriodictis and Protocyon, includes T. platensis Mercerat, 1891; T. tarijenis (F. Ameghino, 1902); P. orcesi Hoffstetter, 1952; P. scagliarum J. L. Kraglievich, 1952; and P. troglodytes (Lund, 1839b), and is closely related to the South American foxes Dusicyon and Pseudalopex (including Lycalopex). This group also entered South America sometime during the late Pliocene or early Pleistocene and radiated into the southern portion of the continent.

The Maned Wolf Chrysocyon, recognized as the sister taxon of Canis, represents the third large-canid lineage. This genus is recorded from the Pleistocene in Bolivia, Brazil, and Argentina. The more extensive present-day range of the Maned Wolf indicates subsequent dispersal into Paraguay and northern Argentina.

In South America during the Pleistocene, the large canids and Felis ecologically replaced the predaceous dog-like marsupial family Borhyaenidae. Members of the Canis and Theriodictis-Protocyon lineages occupied the large to intermediate-sized carnivore adaptive zone during the Pleistocene. Large cats, including Felis onca, F. concolor, and the sabertooth Smilodon were additional occupants of this zone. Pleistocene extinction of the large canids and sabercats, and decline of the large felids, is related to extinction of the large ungulates, prey of these large predators. Today, the jaguar and puma survive as the sole occupants of this zone.

During the Pleistocene, the large-omnivore zone was occupied by the Maned Wolf Chrysocyon, the bear Arctodus, and the procyonids <u>Cyonasua</u>, <u>Brachynasua</u>, and <u>Chapalmalania</u>.   Present-day occupants of this zone include only <u>Chrysocyon</u> and the spectacled bear <u>Tremarctos</u>.

Pleistocene occupants of the small-sized carnivore-omnivore zone include, among the canids, the bush dog <u>Speothos</u>, the small-eared dog <u>Atelocynus</u>, and the foxes <u>Cerdocyon</u> and <u>Pseudalopex</u>.   Members of the Felidae, Procyonidae, and Mustelidae are additional occupants of this zone.

Literature Cited

Allen, J. A.
    1885 On an extinct type of dog from Ely Cave, Lee County,
            Virginia. Mem. Mus. Comp. Zool., Harvard, 10(2):1-13.
    1914 The generic names Speothos and Icticyon. Proc. Biol. Soc.,
            Wash., 27:147.
Ameghino, C.
    1917 Sobre el perro fosil del genero Palaeocyon. Physis (Rev.
            Soc. Argent. Cien. Nat.) 3(4):268.
Ameghino, F.
    1875 Ensayos para servir de base a un estudio de la formacion
            pampeana. Mercedes: La Aspiracion.
    1881 La antiguedad del hombre en La Plata. Paris and Buenos
            Aires. 2 vols.; 600 pp., 700 figs., 25 plates. Republished
            1918.
    1882 Catalogo explicative de las colecciones de antropologia
            prehistorica y de paleontologia de Florentino Ameghino.
            In Catalogo ... de la provencia de Buenos Aires, en la
            Exposition continental de Sudamerica, pp. 35-42.
    1889 Contribucion al conocimiento de los mamiferos fosiles de
            la Republica Argentina, ... para presentarla a la
            Exposicion Universal de Paris de 1889. Actas Acad. Cien.,
            Cordoba, 6:1-1027; atlas, 98 plates.
    1898 Sinopsis geologico-paleontologia. In Segundo censo de la
            Republica Argentina, vol. 1:112-255.

1902　Notas sobre algunos mamiferos fosiles nuevos o poco
　　　conocidos del valle de Tarija. An. Mus. Nac. Buenos
　　　Aires (ser. 3, vol. 1):225-261.

1904　Nuevas especies de mamiferos cretaceos y terciarias de la
　　　Republica Argentina. An. Soc. Cien. Argent. 56-58:1-142.

1905　La perforacion astragaliana en los mamiferos no es un
　　　caracter originariamente primitivo. An. Mus. Nac. Buenos
　　　Aires (ser. 3, vol. 4):344-460.

1906　Les formations sedimentaires du Cretace superieur et du
　　　Tertiare de Patagonie. An. Mus. Nac. Buenos Aires (ser.
　　　3, vol. 8):1-568.

1909　Las formaciones sedimentarios de la region litoral de Mar
　　　del Plata y Chapalmalan. An. Mus. Nac. Buenos Aires
　　　(ser. 3, vol. 10):343-428.

American Commission on Stratigraphic Nomenclature

1961　Code of stratigraphic nomenclature. Amer. Assoc. Petrol.
　　　Geol. Bull. 45950:645-66.

Baskin, J.

1978　Bensonomys, Calomys, and the origin of the phyllotine
　　　group of Neotropical cricetines (Rodentia: Cricetidae).
　　　Jour. Mammalogy, 59:125-135.

Bechstein, J.

1797　Thomas Pennant's allgemeine Ubersicht der vierfussigen
　　　Thiere. Weimar 1:1-320.

Berggren, W. A., and J. A. VanCouvering

1974　The late Neogene. Palaeogeog., Palaeoclimat.,
　　　Palaeoecol. 16(1/2):1-216.

Berta, A.

1981　Evolution of large canids in South America. In Anais II
　　　Congreso Latino-Americano de Paleontologia, Porto Alegre,
　　　vol. 2:835-845.

1982　Cerdocyon thous. Mammalian Species Series no. 186:1-4.
　　　American Society of Mammalogists.

1984   The Pleistocene bush dog _Speothos pacivorus_ (Canidae)
       from the Lagoa Santa Caves, Brazil. Jour. Mammalogy,
       65(4):549-559.

Berta, A., and L. G. Marshall
    1978   Fossilium catalogus I: South American Carnivora. W. Junk
           (The Hague), Pars 125; pp 1-48.

Blainville, H. M. D. de
    1841   Osteographie ou description iconographique comparee du
           squelette et du systeme dentaire des mamiferes recent et
           fossiles pour servir de base a la zoologie et a la
           geologie. Paris (Des petits-ours (G. _Subursus_, livraison
           9): 123 pp.
    1843   Osteographie ou description iconographique comparee du
           squelette et du systeme dentaire des mamiferes recent et
           fossiles pour servir de base a la zoologie et a la
           geologie. Paris (Des _Canis_, livraison 13):160 pp.

Boule, M., and A. Thevenin
    1920   Mammiferes fossiles de Tarija. Miss. Sci. Crequi-
           Montfort et E. S. de la grange. Paris:Soudier. 255 pp.

Bocquentin, M. Jean
    1979   Mammiferes fossiles du Pleistocene superieur de Muaco,
           etat de Falcon, Venezuela. Ph.D. diss., University of
           Paris, vols. 1 and 2; 112 pp. and plates.

Bowdich, T. E.
    1821   An analysis of the natural classifications of Mammalia
           for the use of students and travellers. Paris: J. Smith.
           115 pp.

Bryan, A.
    1973 Paleoenvironments and cultural diversity in late Pleisto-
         cene South America. Quat. Res. 3:237-256.

Bueler, L. E.
    1973 Wild Dogs of the World. New York:Stein and Day. 274 pp.

Burmeister, E.

   1864   La paleontologia actual en sus tendencias y sus
          resultados. An. Mus. Nac. Buenos Aires 1:12-31.

   1879   Description physique de la Republique Argentina d'pres
          des observationes personelles et etrangeres, trans. E.
          Daireaux(from German), vol. 3. Animaux vertebres, part
          1. Mammiferes vivants et eteints, pp. 1-556. Buenos
          Aires.

   1885   Examen critico de los mamiferos y reptiles fosiles
          denominados por D. August Bravard y mencionados en su
          obra precedente. An. Mus. Nac. Buenos Aires 3:95-174.

Cabrera, A.

   1932   El perro cimarron de la Pampa Argentina. Publ. Mus.
          Antropol. y Ethnogr. ...de Buenos Aires (A):7-29.

Churcher, C. S.

   1959   Fossil Canis from the tar pits of La Brea, Peru. Science
          130:564-565.

   1962   Odocoileus salinae and Mazama sp. from the tar seeps,
          Peru. Contrib. Roy. Ontario Mus., Life Sci. div.,
          57:3-27.

   1965   Camelid material of the genus Palaeoloama Gervais from
          the Talara tar seeps, Peru, with a description of a new
          subgenus Astylolama. Proc. Zool. Soc. London 145:161-205.

Churcher, C. S., and C. G. Van Zyll de Jong

   1965   Conepatus talarae n. sp. from the Talara tar-seeps, Peru.
          Contrib. Roy. Ontario Mus., Life Sci. div., 62:1-15.

Clutton-Brock, J., G. B. Corbet, and M. Hills

   1976   A review of the family Canidae, with a classification by
          numerical methods. Bull. Brit. Mus. (Nat. Hist.)
          29(3):120-199.

Croizat, L., G. Nelson, and D. E. Rosen

   1974   Centers of origin and related concepts. Syst. Zool.
          23:265-287.

Desmarest, A. G.

1820 Mammalogie du description des especes de mammiferes.
      part. 1. Ordres des Bimanes, des Quadrumanes, et des
      Carnassiers. Paris. 276 pp.

Doering, A.

1882 Informe official de la Comission cientifica ...de la
      expedicion al Rio Negro, etc., vol. 3:299-530. Buenos
      Aires.

Downs, T.

1958 Fossil vertebrates from Lago de Chapal, Jalisco, Mexico.
      20th Internat. Geol. Congr., Mexico, 1956, publ. 7:75-77.

Eldredge, N., and J. Cracraft

1980 Phylogenetic Patterns and the Evolutionary Process. New
      York:Columbia University Press. 349 pp.

Evans, H. E., and G. C. Christensen

1979 Miller's Anatomy of the Dog. Philadelphia:Saunders.
      1181 pp.

Evernden, J. F., S. F. Kritz, and C. Cherroni

1966 Correlaciones de las formaciones terciarias de la cuenca
      altiplantica a base de edades absolutas, determinadas por
      el metido Potasio-Argon. Serv. Geol. Bolivia, Hoja Inf.,
      no. 1.

Evernden, J. F., D. E. Savage, G. H. Curtis, and G. T. James

1964 Potassium-argon dates and the Cenozoic mammalian
      chronology of North America. Amer. J. Sci. 262:145-198.

Ewer, R. F.

1973 The Carnivores. New York:Cornell University Press.
      494 pp.

Frenguelli, J.

1928 Sobre un resto de canido del Chapalmalense de Miramar.
      An. Fac. Cien. Educ. Univ. Litoral Argent., 3:195-207.

1929 Canis (Macrocyon) chapalmalensis n. sp. An. Soc. Cien.
      Argent. 107:58-65.

Furlong, E. L.
    1925 Notes on the occurrence of mammalian remains in the
          Pleistocene of Mexico, with a description of a new
          species Capromeryx mexicana. Univ. Calif. Publ. Geol.
          Sci. 15(5):137-152.

Gaspard, M.
    1964 La region de l'angle mandibulaire chez les Canidae.
          Mammalia 28:249-329.

Gervais, H., and F. Ameghino
    1880 Les mammiferes fossiles de l'Amerique du Sud. Buenos
          Aires and Paris. xi + 225 pp.

Giebel, C. G.
    1855 Die Saugethiere in zoologisher, anatomischer, und
          palaeontologischer Beziehung umfassend dargestellt.
          Leipzig. xii + 1108 pp.

Gill, T.
    1872 Arrangement of the families of mammals with analytical
          tables. Smithsonian Misc. Coll. 11(1):1-98.

Gray, J. E.
    1821 On the natural arrangement of vertebrose animals. London
          Med. Reposit. 15(1):296-310.

    1846 On a new genus of dogs. Ann. Mag. Nat. Hist. 17:193-194.
Hamilton Smith, C.
    1839 Natural history of dogs, vol. 1. The naturalist's
          library (W. Jardine, ed.). W. H. Lizars, Edinburgh,
          18:1-267 pp.

Harrington, H. J.
    1956 Argentina. In Handbook of South American Geology, ed. W.
          F. Jenks pp. 136-165. Geol. Soc. Amer. Mem. 65:1378.
Hecht, M.
    1976 Phylogenetic inference and methodology as applied to the
          vertebrate record. In Evolutionary Biology, ed. T.
          Dobzhansky, M. Hecht, and W. Steere, vol. 9:335-363. New
          York:Appleton-Century-Crofts.

Hecht, M., and J. L. Edwards
    1976   The determination of parallel or monophyletic
           relationships and the proteid salamanders-a test case.
           Amer. Nat. 110(974):653-677.
Henning, W.
    1966   Phylogenetic Systematics.   Urbana:University of Illinois
           Press: 263 pp.
Hershkovitz, P.
    1958   A geographical classification of neotropical mammals:
           Fieldiana (Zool.) 36(6):581-620.
    1962   Evolution of neotropical cricetine rodents (Muridae),
           with special reference to the phyllotine group.
           Fieldiana (Zool.) 46:1-427.
    1966   Mice, land bridges, and the Latin American faunal
           interchange.   In Ectoparasites of Panama, ed. R. L.
           Wenzel and V. J. Tipton, pp. 725-751.   Chicago:Field
           Museum of Natural History.
    1969   The evolution of mammals on southern continents, VI.   The
           Recent mammals of the Neotropical Region: a zoogeographic
           and ecological review.   Quart. Rev. Biol. 44(1):1-70.
    1972   The Recent mammals of the Neotropical Region: a
           zoogeographic and ecologic review.   In Evolution,
           Mammals, and Southern Continents, ed. A. Keast, F. C.
           Erk, and B. Glass, pp. 311-431.   Albany:State University
           of New York Press, Albany, New York Press.
Hildebrand, M.
    1952   An analysis of body proportions in the Canidae.   Amer.
           Jour. Anat. 90:217-256.
Hirschfeld, S. E.
    1981   Pliometanastes protistus (Edentata, Megalonychidae) from
           Knight's Ferry, California, with discussion of early
           Hemphillian megalonychids.   PaleoBios 36:1-16.

Hoffstetter, R. J.

  1949   Sobre los Megatheriidae de Pleistoceno del Ecuador:
         Schaubia gen. nov. Bol. Inf. Cien. Nac. 3(25)
         suppl.:1-45, figs. 1-10.

  1952   Les mammiferes pleistocenes de la Republique de
         l'Equateur. Mem. Soc. Geol. France, n.s., 31(66):1-391.
         110 figs., 8 plates., 27 tables.

  1963a La faune pleistocene de Tarija (Bolivie), note
         preliminaire. Bull. Mus. Nat. Hist. Paris 35(2):194-203.

  1963b Les Glyptodontes du Pleistocene de Tarija (Bolivie), I.
         Genres Hoplophorus et Panochthus. Bull. Soc. Geol. France
         5:126-133.

  1968   Nuapua, un gisement de vertebres pleistocene dans le
         chaco bolivien. Bull. Mus. Nat. Hist. Paris 40:823-836.

  1970   Vertebrados cenozoicos y mamiferos cretacios de Peru. In
         Act. IV Congr. Latin Zool. (1969), vol. 2:971-983.

Hoffstetter, R. J., and C. Villarroel

  1974   Decouverte d'un Marsupial Microtragulide (=Argyrolagidae)
         dans le Pliocene de l'altiplano boliven. C. R. Acad.
         Sci. Paris (ser. D) 278:1947-1950.

Hough, J. R.

  1948   The auditory region in some members of the Procyonidae,
         Canidae, and Ursidae: its significance in the phylogeny
         of the Carnivora. Bull. Amer. Mus. Nat. Hist.
         92(2):70-118.

Huxley, T. H.

  1880   On the cranial and dental characters of the Canidae.
         Proc. Zool. Soc. London 16:238-288.

Illiger, K.

  1815   Uberblick der Saugethiere nach ihrer Verteilung uber die
         Welttheile. Abh. K. Akad. Wiss. Berlin 1804-1811,
         pp. 39-159.

Jacobs, L.
    1977 Rodents of the Hemphillian age Redington local fauna, San
          Pedro Valley, Arizona. Jour. Paleontol. 51:505-519.
Keast, A.
    1972 Comparisons of contemporary mammal faunas of southern
          continents. In Evolution, Mammals and Southern
          Continents, ed. A. Keast, F. C. Erk, and B. Glass, pp.
          433-501. Albany:State University of New York Press.
    1977 Zoogeography and Phylogeny: the theoretical background
          and methodology to the analysis of mammal and bird
          faunas. In Major Patterns in Vertebrate Evolution, ed. M.
          K. Hecht, P. C. Goody, and B. M. Hecht, pp. 249-312. New
          York:Plenum Press.
Keigwin, L. D., Jr.
    1978 Pliocene closing of the isthmus of Panama, based on
          biostratigraphic evidence from nearby Pacific Ocean and
          Caribbean Sea cores. Geology 6:630-634.
    1982 Isotopic paleooceanography of the Caribbean and east
          Pacific: role of Panama uplift in late Neogene time.
          Science 217:350-353.
Kerr, R.
    1792 The animal kingdom or zoological system of ... C.
          Linneaus: Class I. Mammalia (Class II. Birds), being a
          translation of that part of the Systema Naturae as
          published by Prof. Gmelin. 2 parts, xii+ 644 pp.,
          London.
Kisko, L. M.
    1967 A consideration of the dire wolves from the New World
          Pleistocene, with a statistical study of their meta-
          podials. M. Sci. thesis, University of Toronto. 75 pp.
Kraglievich, J. L.
    1952 Un canido del Eocuartario de Mar del Plata y sus
          relaciones con otras formas brasilenas y norteamericanas.
          Rev. Mus. Mun. Cien. Nat. Trad. Mar del Plata 1:53-70.

1959 Contribucion al conocimiento de la geologia cuartaria en
      la Argentina. IV Com. Mus. Argent. Cien. Nat. "B.
      Rivadavia" 1(17):1-19.

Kraglievich, L.

1917 Notas paleontologicas: Examen critico de un trabajo del
      Senor Alcides Mercerat. An. Soc. Cien. Argent.
      83:262-279.

1928 Contribucion al conocimiento de los grandes canidos
      extinguidos de Sud America. An. Soc. Cien. Argent.
      106:35-66.

1929 Sobre la auscencia natural de metaconido en el M_1 de
      Canis moreni Lydek. y otras cuestiones. An. Soc. Cien.
      Argent. 107:243-254.

1930 Craneometria y clasificacion de los canidos
      sudamericanos, especialmente los argentinos actuales y
      fosiles. Physis (Rev. Soc. Argent. Cien. Nat.) 10:35-73.

1934 La antiguedad pliocena de las faunas de Monte Hermoso y
      Chapadmalal, deduciadas de su comparacion con las que le
      precedieron y sucedieron. El Siglo Ilustrado
      (Montevideo) 938:1-136.

Kurten, B.

1967 Pleistocene bears of North America, 2. Genus Arctodus,
      short-faced bears. Acta Zool. Fenn. 117:1-60.

1968 Pleistocene mammals of Europe. Chicago:Aldine. 316 pp.

Langguth, A.

1969 Die sudamerikanischen Canidae unter besonderer
      Berucksichtigung des Mahnenwolfes Chrysocyon brachyurus
      Illiger. Zeitschr. Wiss. Zool. 179:1-88.

1975 Ecology and evolution in the South American canids. In
      The Wild Canids, ed. M. W. Fox, pp. 192-206. New
      York:Van Nostrand Reinhold.

Leidy, J.

1858 Notice of remains of extinct vertebrata from the valley
      of the Niobrara River, collected during the exploring

expedition of 1857, in Nebraska ... by F. Hayden. Proc.
Acad. Nat. Sci., Philadelphia, pp. 20-29.

Lemon, R. R. H., and C. S. Churcher
  1961 Pleistocene geology and paleontology of the Talara
        region, northwest Peru. Amer. Jour. Sci. 259:410-429.

Lindsay, E. H., N. M. Johnson, and N. D. Opdyke
  1976 Preliminary correlation of North American land mammal
        ages and geomagnetic chronology. In Studies on Cenozoic
        Paleontology and Stratigraphy in Honor of C. W. Hibbard
        pp. 111-119. Univ. Michigan Papers on Paleontology no.
        12.

Linnaeus, C.
  1758 Systema naturae per regna tria naturae, secundum classes,
        ordines, genera, species cum characteribus, differentiis,
        synonymis, locis, 10th rev. ed., vol. 1. Stockholm.
        824 pp.

Lund, P. W.
  1839a Blik paa Brasiliens Dyreverden for sidste
        jordomvaeltning. Anden Afh. Pattedyrene. Lagoa Santa,
        Nov. 16, 1837. pp. 1-34. Danske Vidensk. Selsk.
        Naturv. Mathem. Afdel. 8:61-144, plates 1-13. (Portugese
        trans. P. W. Lund, 1950, chap. 4, pp. 131-203.)

  1839b Coup d'oeil sur les especes eteintes de Mammiferes du
        Bresil; extrait de quelques memoires presentes a
        l'Academie royale de Copenhague. Lagoa Santa, Nov. 5,
        1838. Ann. Sci. Nat. (Paris) (ser. 2, vol. 11):214-234).
        (Portugese trans. P. W. Lund, 1950. chap. 6:251-269).

  1840a Blik paa Brasiliens Dyreverden for sidste
        jordomvaeltning. Tredie Afhandling: Fortsaettelse af
        Pattedyrene. Lagoa Santa, Sept. 12, 1838. Copenhagen.
        156 pp. Danske Vidensk. Selsk Naturv. Mathem. Afdel.,
        8:27-144. (Portugese trans. P. W. Lund, 1950, chap.
        5:207-250).

1840b Nouvelles recherches sur la faune fossile du Bresil.
       Ann. Sci. Nat. (Paris) (ser.2, vol. 13) 310-319.
       (Portugese trans. P. W. Lund. 1950, chap. 9, pp.
       307-316).

1842   Blik paa Brasiliens Dyreverden for sidste
       jordomvaeltning. Fjerde Afhandling: Fortsaettelse af
       Pattedyrene. Lagoa Santa, Jan. 30, 1841. Copenhagen. 72
       pp. Danske Vidensk. Selsk. Naturv. Mathem. Afdel.
       9:137-208, plates 28-38. (Portugese trans. P. W. Lund,
       1950, chap. 10:317-377).

1843   Blik paa Brasiliens Dyreverden for sidste
       jordomvaeltning. Fjerde Afhandling: Om de nulvende og
       uddode arter af Rovdyrenes Families. Lagoa Santa, Oct.
       4, 1841. Copenhagen. Danske Vidensk. Selsk. Naturv.
       Mathem. Afdel. 9:1-82, plates 40-46. (Portugese trans.
       P. W. Lund, 1950, chap. 11 pp. 381-455).

Lydekker, R.
    1894 On two Argentine extinct carnivores. Anal. Mus. La Plata
          3:1-4.

MacFadden, B. J., O. Siles, P. Zeitler, N. M. Johnson, and K. E.
       Campbell, Jr.
    1983 Magnetic polarity stratigraphy of the middle Pleistocene
          (Ensenadan) Tarija formation of southern Bolivia. Quat.
          Res. 19(2):172-187.

MacFadden, B. J., and R. G. Wolff
    1981 Geological investigations of late Cenozoic
          vertebrate-bearing deposits in southern Bolivia. In
          Anais II Congreso Latino-Americano de Paleontologia,
          Porto Alegre, vol. 2:765-778.

Maldonado, M.
    1955 Sobre un craneo de Aenocyon dirus (Leidy) del Pleistoceno
          superior de Tequixquiac, Mexico. Inst. Nac. Antrop. Hist.
          Mexico 36:51-58.

Marshall, L. G.
    1978 Evolution of the Borhyaenidae, extinct South American
          predaceous marsupials. Univ. Calif. Publ. Geol. Sci.
          117:1-89.
    1979a Evolution of the carnivorous adaptive zone in South
          America, pp. 709-721. NATO Advanced Study Institute. New
          York:Plenum Press.
    1979b A model of South American cricetine rodents. Paleobiology
          5(2):126-132.
Marshall, L. G., A. Berta, R. J. Hoffstetter, R. Pascual, O. A.
          Reig, M. Bombin, and A. Mones
    1984 Mammals and Stratigraphy: Geochronology of the
          continental Quaternary mammal record of South America.
          Palaeovertebrata, Mem. Extr.:1-76.
Marshall, L. G., R. F. Butler, R. E. Drake, and G. H. Curtis
    1982 Geochronology of type Uquian (late Cenozoic) land mammal
          age, Argentina. Science 216:986-989.
Marshall, L. G., R. F. Butler, R. Pascual, R. E. Drake, G. H.
          Curtis, and R. H. Tedford
    1979 Calibration of the Great American Interchange. Science
          204 (4390):272-279.
Martin, R. A.
    1974 Fossil mammals from the Coleman IIA Fauna, Sumter County.
          In Pleistocene Mammals of Florida, ed. S. D. Webb, pp.
          35-99. Gainesville: University of Florida Press.
Mercerat, A.
    1891 Caracteres diagnosticos de algunas especies de Creodonta
          conservados en el Museo de La Plata Rev. Mus. La Plata,
          2:51-56.
    1917a Notas sobre algunos carnivoros fosiles y actuales de la
          America del Sud. 14 pp. Buenos Aires: R. Herrando y
          Cia, impresores.
    1917b Adicion a las notas sobre carnivoros fosiles; pp. 15-21.
          Buenos Aires: R. Herrando y Cia, impresores.

Merriam, J. C.

  1912 The fauna of Rancho La Brea, Part. 2. Canidae. Mem.
        Univ. Calif. 1(2):215-272.

  1918 Note on the systematic position of the wolves of the
        Canis dirus group. Univ. Calif. Bull. Dept. Geol.
        10:531-533.

Mooser, O., and W. Dalquest

  1975 Pleistocene mammals from Aguascalientes, central Mexico.
        Jour. Mammalogy 56(4):781-820.

Nehring, A.

  1885 Die Schadelform und das Gebiss des Canis jubatus
        Desmarest (C. campestris Pr. Wied). Sitz-Berlin Ges.
        Naturf. Freunde, Berlin, pp. 109-122.

Nelson, G.

  1978 Ontogeny, phylogeny, paleontology, and the biogenic law.
        Syst. Zool. 27(3):324-345.

Nowak, R. M.

  1979 North American Quaternary Canis. Univ. Kansas Mus. Nat.
        Hist. Monog. 6:1-154.

Nygren, W. E.

  1950 Bolivar geosyncline of northwestern South America. Bull.
        Amer. Assoc. Petrol. Geol. 34(10):1998-2006.

Osgood, W. H.

  1919 Names of some South American Mammals. Jour. Mammalogy
        1:33-38.

Palmer, T. S.

  1904 Index Generum Mammalium: A list of the genera and
        families of mammals. USDA, North American Fauna
        23:1-984.

Parodiz, J. J.

  1969 The Tertiary non-marine Mollusca of South America. Ann.
        Carnegie Mus. 40:1-242.

Pascual, R., E. J. O. Hinojosa, D. Goudar, and E. Tonni
   1966 Paleontografia Bonaerense, IV. Vertebrata. Com. Invest.
         Cien. Prov. Buenos Aires, La Plata.

Pascual, R., E. J. O. Hinojosa, D. Goudar, and E. Tonni
   1967 Les edades del Cenozoico mammalifero de la Argentina, con
         especial atencion a aquellas del territorio bonaraerense.
         An. Com. Invest. Cien. Buenos Aires, pp. 165-193.

Pascual, R., and O. Rivas
   1971 Evolucion de las comunidades de los vertebrados del
         Terciario Argentina: los aspectos paleozoogeograficos y
         paleoclimaticos relacionados. Ameghiniana 8:373-412.

   1973 Las unidades estratigraficas del Terciario portadores de
         mamiferos: su distribution y sus relaciones con los
         acontecimientos diastroficos. In Actas del Quinto
         Congreso Geologico Argentino, vol. 3:293-338.

Patterson, B., and F. Fidalgo
   1972 The problem of the Plio-Pleistocene boundary in Argentina
         (South America). In Internat. Colloquium on the Boundary
         between Neogene and Quaternary, Moscow, pp. 205-262.

Patterson, B., and R. Pascual
   1972 The fossil mammal fauna of South America. In Evolution,
         Mammals, and Southern Continents, ed. A. Keast, F. C.
         Erk, and B. Glass, pp. 247-309. Albany:State University
         of New York Press.

Paula Couto, C. de
   1946 Atualizacao da nomenclatura generica e expecifica usada
         por Herlut Winge. Museo Lundii 1(3):59-80.

Repenning, C. A.
   1967 Palearctic-Nearactic mammalian dispersal in the late
         Cenozoic. In The Bering Land Bridge, ed. D. M. Hopkins,
         pp. 288-314. Stanford, Calif.:Stanford University Press.

Revilliod, P.
   1924a Les grands chiens quaternaires de l'Amerique du Sud; note
         preliminaire. Ecologae Geol. Helvetiae 19:170.

1924b Note preliminaire sur le *Canis morenoi* Lydekker. C. R.
      Soc. Hist. Nat. Geneve 41(1):11-12.

1926 Etude critique sure les genres de Canides quaternaires
      sudamericaines et description d'un crane de *Palaeocyon*.
      Abh. schweiz. pal. Ges. 44(2):1-14.

Riggs, E. S., and B. Patterson

1939 Stratigraphy of late Miocene and Pliocene deposits of the
      province of Catamarca (Argentina), with notes on the
      faunae. Physis 14:143-162.

Royo y Gomez. J.

1960 El yacimiento de vertebrados Pleistocenos Muaco, estado
      de Falcon, Venezuela, con industria lithica humana. In
      Proc. 21st Internat. Geol. Congress, 1960, sect. 4,
      Norden, Copenhagen.

Rusconi, C.

1929 Enumeracion sistematica de las especies de mamiferos
      procedentes del piso ensenadense hallados por el autor.
      Buenos Aires: privately printed, M. L. Rano. 15 pp.

1931 Lista de los vertebrados fosiles del Pliocene superior
      de Buenos Aires. La Seman Medica, 53:1-19 (of reprint).

1936 Distribucion de los vertebrados fosiles del piso
      ensenadense. Bol. Acad. Nac. Cien. Cordoba 33:183-215.

Russell, R.

1960 Pleistocene pocket gophers from San Josecito Cave, Nuevo
      Leon, Mexico. Univ. Kansas Mus. Nat. Hist. Publ.
      9:539-548.

Savage, J. M.

1974 The isthmian link and the evolution of Neotropical
      mammals. Los Angeles Co. Mus. Contrib. Sci. 260:1-51.

Schinz, A.

1848 Note sur un nouveau genre de mammifere repace du Bresil.
      Rev. Zoo. Soc. Cuvierienne 11:176-178.

Simpson, G. G.

    1931 A new classification of mammals. Bull. Amer. Mus. Nat.
          Hist. 59:259-293.

    1941 Large Pleistocene felines of North America. Amer. Mus.
          Nov. 1136:1-27.

    1945 The principles of classification and a classification of
          mammals. Bull. Amer. Mus. Nat. Hist. 85:1-35.

    1950 History of the fauna of Latin America. Amer. Jour.
          Sci. 38:361-389.

    1962 Evolution and geography: an essay on historical
          biogeography, with special reference to mammals.
          University of Oregon Press. 64 pp.

    1972 Didelphidae from the Chapadmalal Formation in the Museo
          Municipal de Ciencias Naturales of Mar del Plata. Publ.
          Mus. Munic. Cien. Nat. Mar del Plata, 2(1):1-39.

    1980 Splendid Isolation. Yale University Press. 266 pp.

Spillmann, F.

    1941 Uber einen neuen hydrochoeren Riesennager zus dem
          Pleistozan von Ekuador. Journ. Geol. Soc. Japan
          48(571):196-201.

    1942 Contribucion al conocimiento de fosiles nuevos de la
          avifauna equatoriana en el Pleistoceno de Santa Elena.
          In Proc. 8th Amer. Sci. Congr., vol. 4:375-389.

    1948 Beitrage zur Kenntnis eines neuen gravigraden
          Riesensteppentieres (Eremotherium carolinense gen. et sp.
          nov.), seines Lebensraumes und seiner Lebensweise.
          Palaeobio. 1(8):231-279.

Stock, C., J. F. Lance, and J. O. Nigra

    1946 A newly mounted skeleton of the extinct dire wolf from
          the Pleistocene of Rancho La Brea. Bull. So. Calif.
          Acad. Sci. 45 (part 2):108-110.

Tedford, R. H.

    1968 A review of the phylogeny and classification of the Order
          Carnivora (Mammalia). Unpub. ms.

Thenius, E.

  1954 Zur Abstammung der Rotwolfe (Gattung Cuon Hodgson)
        Osterreichische Zoologishe Zeitschrift 5(3):378-387.

  1970 Einige jungpleistozane Saugetiere (Platygonus, Arctodus,
        und Canis dirus) aus dem Valsequillo, Mexiko. Quartar Bd.
        21:57-66.

Torre, D.

  1979 The Ruscinian and the Villafranchian dogs of Europe. Bol.
        Soc. Paleont. Ital. 18(2):162-165.

Torres, R. V., and I. Ferrusquia V.

  1981 Cerdocyon sp. nov. A (Mammalia, Carnivora) en Mexico y su
        significacion evolutiva y zoogeografica en relacion a los
        canidos sudamericanos.   In Anais II Congreso
        Latino-Americano de Paleontologia, Porto Alegre, vol.
        2:709-719.

Trouessart, E. L.

  1898 Catalogus mammalium tam viventium quam fossilium, new
        ed., vol. 11:665-1265. Berlin.

  1904 Catalogus mammalium tam viventium quam fossilium, suppl.
        5. Berlin. 929 pp.

Troxell, E. L.

  1915 The vertebrate fossils of Rock Creek, Texas. Amer. Jour.
        Sci. 39(234):612-638.

Turnbull, W. D.

  1978 Another look at dental specialization in the extinct
        saber-toothed marsupial Thylacosmilus, compared with its
        placental counterparts. In Development, Function, and
        Evolution of Teeth, ed. K. A. Joysey, pp. 349-414,
        London:Academic Press.

Van Valen, L.

  1966 The Deltatheridia, a new order of mammals. Bull. Amer.
        Mus. Nat. Hist. 132:1-126.

  1971 Adaptive zones and the orders of mammals. Evolution
        25:328-420.

Watrous, L. E. and Q. D. Wheeler

    1981 The out-group comparison method of character analysis.
          Syst. Zool, 30(1):1-11.

Webb, S. D.

    1976 Mammalian faunal dynamics of the great American
          interchange. Paleobiology 2(3):220-234.

    1978 A history of savanna vertebrates in the New World, Part
          2. South America and the great interchange. Ann. Rev.
          Ecol. Syst. 9:393-426.

Whitmore, F. C., and R. H. Stewart

    1965 Miocene mammals and Central American seaways. Science
          148:180-185.

Wied, M. P.

    1826 Beitrage zur naturgeschichte von Brasilien. Verzeichnis
          der Amphibien Saugethiere und Vogel, welche auf einer
          Reise Zwischen dem 13ten und dem 23ten Grade sudlicher
          Breite im ostlichen Brasilien beobachtet wurden II.
          Abteilung. Mammalia. Saugethiere - Weimar, vol. 2:1-620.

Wiley, E. O.

    1975 Karl R. Popper, systematics, and classification: a reply
          to Walter Bock and other evolutionary taxonomists. Syst.
          Zool. 24:233-243.

Winge, H.

    1895 Jordfunde og nulevende Rovdyr (Carnivora) fra Lagoa
          Santa, Minas Geraes, Brasilien. E. Museo Lundii
          2(4):1-103.

Woodring, W. P.

    1966 The Panama land bridge as a sea barrier. Proc. Am.
          Philos. Soc. 110:425-433.

Plates

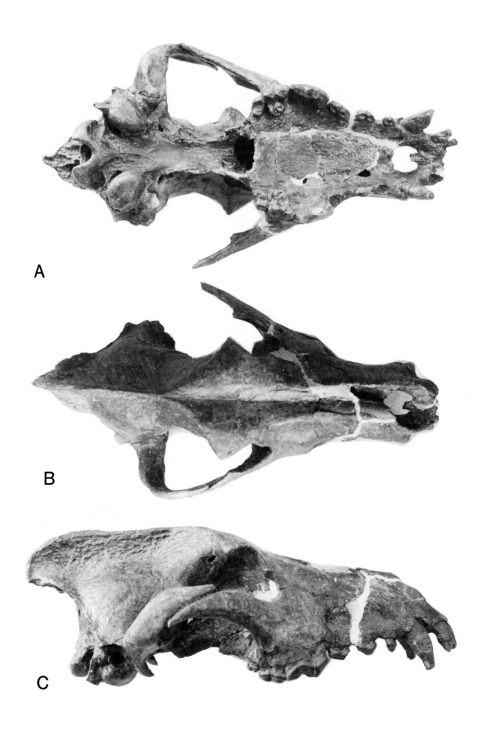

Plate 1. *Canis dirus* Leidy, 1858. VF?, skull: (A) ventral, (B) dorsal, and (C) lateral views. Scale = 30 mm.

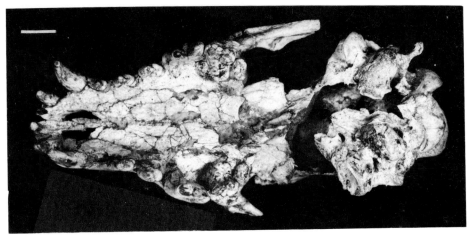

A

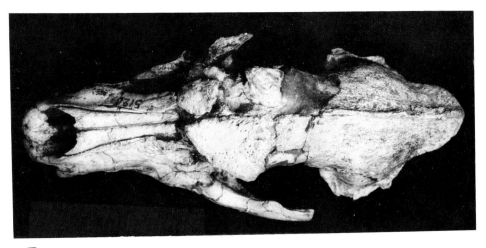

B

Plate 2. <u>Canis gezi</u> L. Kraglievich, 1928. MACN 5120, skull: (A) ventral and (B) dorsal views. Scale = 20 mm.

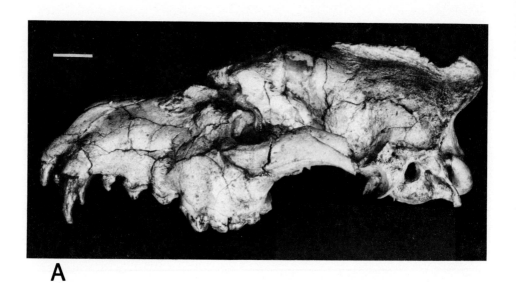

A

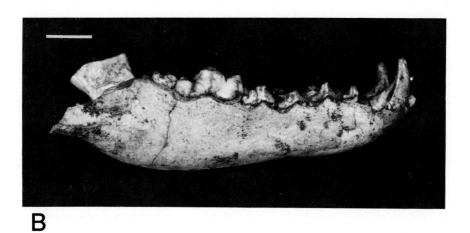

B

Plate 3. <u>Canis</u> <u>gezi</u> L. Kraglievich, 1928. MACN 5120, skull and associated right mandible: (A) and (B) lateral views. Scale = 20 mm.

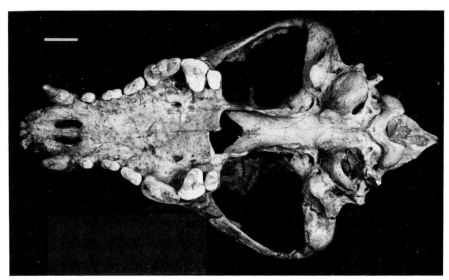

A

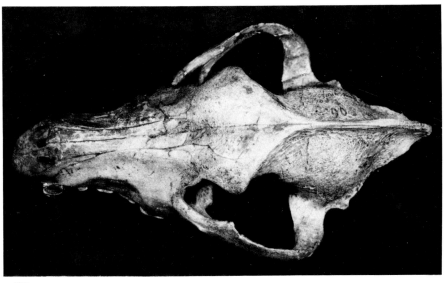

B

Plate 4. <u>Canis</u> <u>nehringi</u> (F. Ameghino, 1902). MACN 500, skull:
(A) ventral and (B) dorsal views. Scale = 20 mm.

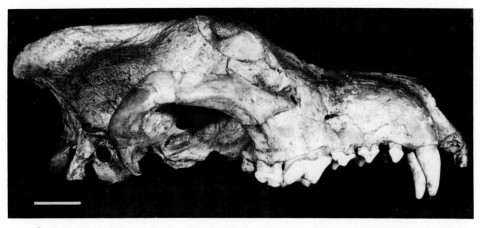

A

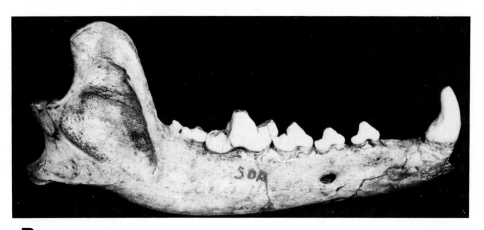

B

Plate 5.   Canis nehringi (F. Ameghino, 1902). MACN 500, skull
          and associated right mandible: (A) and (B) lateral
          views.   Scale = 20 mm.

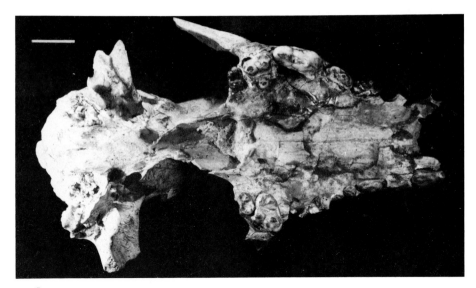

A

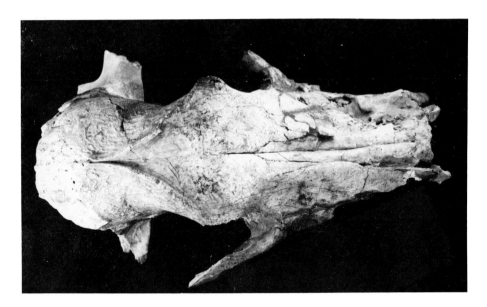

B

Plate 6.   Theriodictis platensis Mercerat, 1891.   MLP 10-51,
          skull: (A) ventral and (B) dorsal views.
          Scale = 30 mm.

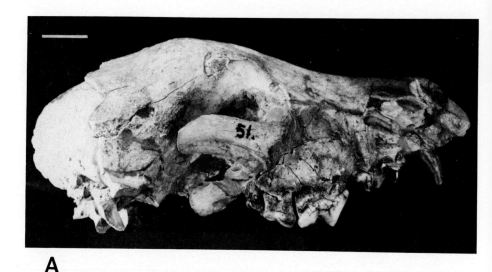

A

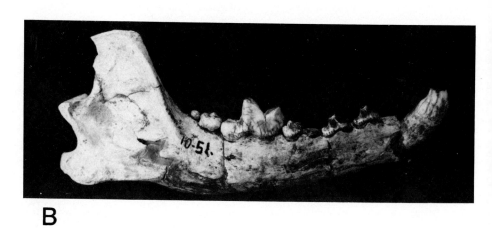

B

Plate 7. Theriodictis platensis Mercerat, 1891. MLP 10-51,
          skull and associated mandible: (A) and (B) lateral
          views. Scale = 20 mm.

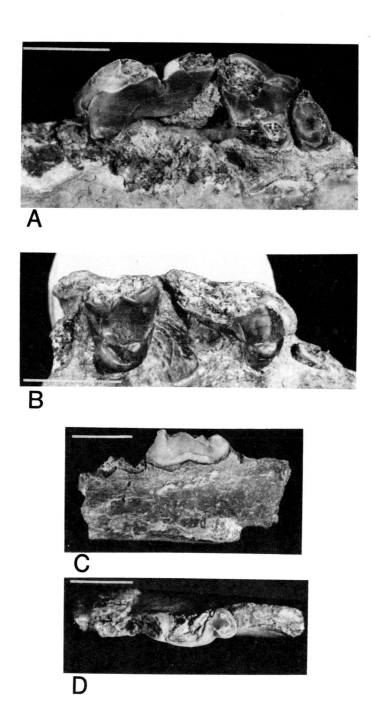

Plate 8. *Theriodictis tarijensis* (F. Ameghino, 1902).
MACN 1452: (A) left maxillary with P^4-M^2,
lingual view; (B) right maxillary with P^4-M^2,
lingual view; associated left ramal fragment with M_1,
(C) lateral and (D) occlusal views. Scale = 20 mm.

A

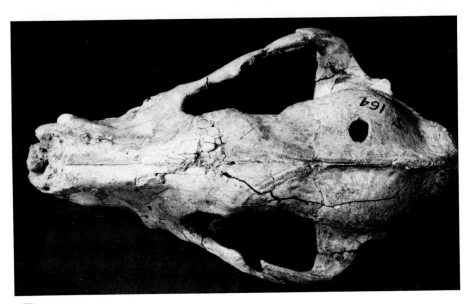

B

Plate 9. Protocyon scagliarum J. L. Kraglievich, 1952. MMP 164,
          skull: (A) ventral and (B) dorsal views.
          Scale = 20 mm.

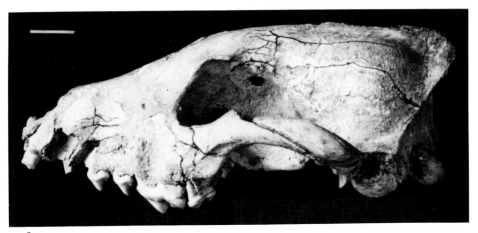

A

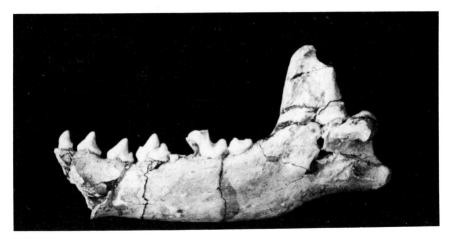

B

Plate 10. <u>Protocyon</u> <u>scagliarum</u> J. L. Kraglievich, 1952. MMP
164, skull and associated right mandible: (A) lateral
and (B) lingual views. Scale = 20 mm.

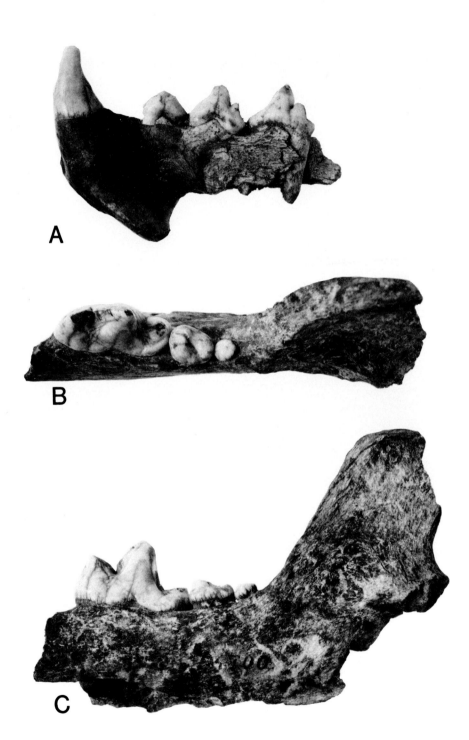

Plate 11. <u>Protocyon troglodytes</u> (Lund, 1839b). (A) UZM L2157, left ramus with C, P_{2-4}, lateral view. UZM L5700, right ramus with M_{1-3}: (B) occlusal and (C) lingual views. Scale = 20 mm.

University of California Press
Berkeley 94720

ISBN 0-520-0